P9-CMY-553

A12900 238847

ILLINOIS CENTRAL COLLEGE
PS614.R53 1971
STACKS
The third book of modern verse;

A12900 238847

PS
614   RITTENHOUSE
.R53   The third b
1971   verse

WITHDRAWN

Illinois Central College
Learning Resource Center

GRANGERS

THE THIRD BOOK
OF MODERN VERSE

THE THIRD BOOK OF
MODERN VERSE

A

SELECTION FROM THE WORK
OF CONTEMPORANEOUS
AMERICAN POETS

EDITED BY
JESSIE B. RITTENHOUSE , *1869-1948*

Granger Index Reprint Series

ILLINOIS CENTRAL COLLEGE
LEARNING RESOURCE CENTER

 BOOKS FOR LIBRARIES PRESS
FREEPORT, NEW YORK

36848

PS
614
.R53
1971

Copyright © 1927 by Jessie Rittenhouse Scollard

Reprinted 1971 by arrangement with
Houghton Mifflin Company

INTERNATIONAL STANDARD BOOK NUMBER:
0-8369-6239-7

LIBRARY OF CONGRESS CATALOG CARD NUMBER:
79-149114

PRINTED IN THE UNITED STATES OF AMERICA

EDITOR'S NOTE
(TO THE ORIGINAL EDITION)

THE material in this book has been, in the main, collected from work published since 1919, the date of publication of *The Second Book of Modern Verse*. The editor has not hesitated, however, to draw upon the earlier verse of a poet when it seemed, in her judgment, to represent him more adequately than his later work.

The editor regrets that restrictions of copyright prevented her from including the work of James Branch Cabell and Maxwell Bodenheim.

JESSIE B. RITTENHOUSE

CONTENTS

CONTENTS

CONTENTS

CONTENTS

CONTENTS

ACKNOWLEDGMENTS

THE editor wishes to express her thanks to the authors and publishers of the poems included in this volume, who have so kindly granted permission for their use. All rights in these poems are reserved by the holders of copyright or the authorized publishers as named below:

D. Appleton and Company, for selections from "Honey Out of the Rock," by Babette Deutch, from "Selected Poems," by Charles Hanson Towne, and from "A Harp in the Winds," by Daniel Henderson.

Brentano's, Inc., for selections from "The Sea and the Dunes," by Harry Kemp, and from "Ulysses Returns and Other Poems," by Roselle Mercier Montgomery.

Bobbs Merrill Company, for a selection from "Collected Poems," by John Erskine (copyright, 1922), and from "Sonata and Other Poems," by John Erskine (copyright, 1925), used by special permission of the publishers.

Boni and Liveright, for selections from "Personæ," by Ezra Pound; "Priapus and the Pool," by Conrad Aiken; "Roan Stallion," by Robinson Jeffers; Collected Poems of H. D.; "White Rooster," by George O'Neil; "Will-o'-the-Wisp," by Dorothy Dow; "White Buildings," by Hart Crane; and "Rock Flower," by Jeanne Robert Foster.

Albert and Charles Boni, for selections from "Tulips and Chimney Pots," by E. E. Cummings; "Spring Thunder" and "7 P.M.," by Mark Van Doren; "Lava Lane," by Nathalia Crane, and "Gypsy Gold," by Charles Divine.

B. J. Brimmer Company, for selections from "Many Wings," by Isabel Fiske Conant.

Nicholas L. Brown, for selections from "A Half Century of Sonnets," by Gustav Davidson.

The Century Company, for selections from "Collected Poems," by Cale Young Rice.

Pascal Covici, Inc., for a selection from "The King of the Black Isles," by J. U. Nicholson.

Dodd Mead and Company, for selections from "Curtains," by Hazel Hall (copyright by Dodd Mead and Company, Inc.).

George H. Doran Company, for selections from volumes copyrighted by them under the following dates: "Vigils," by Aline Kilmer (copyright, 1921); "The Poor King's Daughter," by Aline Kilmer (copyright, 1925); "Black Armor," by Elinor Wylie (copyright, 1923); "The Dancer in the Shrine," by Amanda Benjamin Hall (copyright, 1923); "Tiger Joy," by Stephen Vincent Benét (copyright, 1925); "Selected Poems," by Arthur Davison Ficke (copyright, 1926); "Extenuations," by Edmund Vance Cooke (copyright, 1926); "Selected Poems," by Lizette Woodworth Reese (copyright, 1926); and "Selected Poems," by Amelia Josephine Burr (copyright, 1927).

Dorrance and Company, for a selection from "The Unrisen Morrow," by Mary Sinton Leitch.

Doubleday, Page and Company, for selections from "Parson's Pleasure," by Christopher Morley; from "The Gates of Paradise," by Edwin Markham; and from "Ladders through the Blue," by Hermann Hagedorn.

E. P. Dutton and Company, for selections from "The Earth Turns South," by Clement Wood; "A Canopic Jar," by Leonora Speyer; and "I Sing the Pioneer," by Arthur Guiterman (copyright by E. P. Dutton and Company, New York).

Harcourt, Brace and Company, for selections from volumes copyrighted by them under the following dates: "The New Adam," by Louis Untermeyer (copyright, 1920); "Less Lonely," by Alfred Kreymborg (copyright, 1923); "The American Rhythm," by Mary Austin (copyright, 1923); "Apples Here in My Basket," by Helen Hoyt (copyright, 1924); "The Long Gallery," by Anne Goodwin Winslow (copyright, 1925); "The American Miscellany" (copyright, 1925); "Ballads and Lyrics," by Margaret Widdemer (copyright, 1925); "Not Poppy," by Virginia Moore (copyright, 1926); and "Lilliput," by Roberta Swartz (copyright, 1926).

Harper and Brothers, for selections from volumes copy-

ACKNOWLEDGMENTS xxi

righted by them under the following dates: "Atlas and Beyond," by Elisabeth Coatsworth (copyright, 1924); "Sunrise Trumpets," by Joseph Auslander (copyright, 1924); "Cyclops' Eye," by Joseph Auslander (copyright, 1926); "Color," by Countee Cullen (copyright, 1925); "Animula Vagula," by Leonard Bacon (copyright, 1926); "Selected Poems," of Edith M. Thomas (copyright, 1926); and "Astrolabe," by S. Foster Damon (copyright, 1927).

Henry Holt and Company, for selections from the following volumes copyrighted by them: "New Hampshire," by Robert Frost; "Cornhuskers," by Carl Sandburg; "Slow Smoke," and "Many Many Moons," by Lew Sarett; "Upper Night," by Scudder Middleton; "The Enchanted Mesa," by Glenn Ward Dresbach; "A Cairn of Stars," by Francis Carlin; and "Portraits and Protests," by Sarah N. Cleghorn.

Henry Harrison, for selections from "Touch and Go," by Ralph Cheyney, and from "Dawn Stars," by Lucia Trent.

Houghton Mifflin Company, for selections from "Cups of Illusion," by Henry Bellamann; "An Outland Piper" and "The Tall Men," by Donald Davidson; "Preludes and Symphonies," by John Gould Fletcher; "What's o'Clock," by Amy Lowell; "Streets in the Moon," by Archibald MacLeish; "The Northeast Corner," by Frederick McCreary; "Magic Flame," by Robert Haven Schauffler; and "The Silver Stair," by Abbie Farwell Brown.

Alfred A. Knopf, Inc., for selections from the following volumes, by permission of and special arrangement with Alfred A. Knopf, Inc., authorized publisher: "Caravan," by Witter Bynner; "Flying Fish," and "Ship's Log," by Grace Hazard Conkling; "Poems," by T. S. Eliot; "The Weary Blues," by Langston Hughes; "Airs and Ballads," by John McClure; "Chills and Fever," and "Two Gentlemen in Bonds," by John Crowe Ransom; "Fiddler's Farewell," by Leonora Speyer; "Body and Raiment," by Eunice Tietjens; "Words for the Chisel," by Genevieve Taggard; "The Sea," by James Oppenheim; "The Master-Mistress," by Rose O'Neill; and "Songs of Youth," by Mary Dixon Thayer.

The Macmillan Company, for selections from the following volumes copyrighted by them: "Youth Riding," by Mary Carolyn Davies (copyright, 1919); "Collected Poems," of

Edwin Arlington Robinson (copyright, 1921); "Carolina Chansons," by Hervey Allen and Du Bose Heyward (copyright, 1921); "Collected Poems," of Vachel Lindsay (copyright, 1923); "The Ancient Beautiful Things," by Fannie Stearns Davis (copyright, 1923); "Skylines and Horizons," by Du Bose Heyward (copyright, 1923); "Sea Change," by Muna Lee (copyright, 1923); "Collected Poems," of John G. Neihardt (copyright, 1926); "Selected Poems," of Edgar Lee Masters (copyright, 1925); "Hesperides," by Ridgely Torrence (copyright, 1925); "Mirrors," by Margaret Tod Ritter (copyright, 1925); "Dark of the Moon," by Sara Teasdale (copyright, 1926); "Wide Pastures," by Marie Emile Gilchrist (copyright, 1926); "Eve Walks in her Garden," by Louise Ayres Garnett (copyright, 1926); "Children of the Sun," by James Rorty (copyright, 1926); "Citadels," by Marguerite Wilkinson (copyright, 1926); "Sonnets," by Amory Hare (copyright, 1927); and for the use of "Sweetgrass Range," by Edwin Ford Piper, and "Forgiveness," by Charles O'Donnell.

Robert M. McBride Company for the use of poems from "The Body of This Death," by Louise Bogan.

Edna St. Vincent Millay, for the use of the following poems: "Passer Mortuus Est" and "Elaine" from "Second April," published by Harper and Brothers (copyright, 1921, by Edna St. Vincent Millay); "What Lips My Lips Have Kissed" and "Euclid Alone Has Looked On Beauty Bare," from "The Harp Weaver and Other Poems," published by Harper and Brothers (copyright, 1920, 1921, 1922, and 1923 by Edna St. Vincent Millay).

Thomas B. Mosher, for selections from "Sonnets of the Saints," "Sonnets of the Cross," and "The Voice in the Silence," by Thomas S. Jones, Jr.

The Mosher Press, for selections from "Candle and Cross," by Elisabeth Scollard.

G. P. Putnam's Sons, for selections from "Ships in Harbor," and "Harvest," by David Morton; and "Golden Pheasant," by Kathryn White Ryan (courtesy of G. P. Putnam's Sons, New York and London).

A. M. Robertson of San Francisco, for the use of poems by George Sterling.

Charles Scribner's Sons, for selections from "The Black Panther," by John Hall Wheelock; "Ballads of the Singing Bowl," by Marjorie Allen Seiffert; "When I Grew Up To Middle Age," by Struthers Burt, and "Lute and Furrow," by Olive Tilford Dargan.

Smith and Sale for a selection from "Pagan Sonnets," by John Myers O'Hara.

Frederick A. Stokes Company, for the use of "Lilacs," reprinted by permission from "Shoes of the Wind," by Hilda Conkling (copyright, 1922, by Frederick A. Stokes Company).

Simon and Schuster, for selections from "You Who Have Dreams," by Maxwell Anderson, and "Poems," by Irwin Edman.

Unicorn Press for selections from "Lost Eden," by E. Merrill Root.

Harold Vinal, Inc., for selections from "A Horn from Caerleon," by J. Corson Miller; "The Arrow of Lightning," by Beatrice Ravenel; "Cliff Dwellings," by Glenn Ward Dresbach; "White April," by Harold Vinal; and "Peacocks in the Sun," by Margaret Root Garvin.

The Viking Press, New York, for selections from "Two Lives," by William Ellery Leonard (copyright, 1922 and 1925, by B. W. Huebsch, Inc.); "Sun-Up," by Lola Ridge (copyright, 1920, by B. W. Huebsch, Inc.); and "Red Flag," by Lola Ridge (copyright, 1927, by The Viking Press, New York).

Yale University Press for selections from "Wampum and Old Gold," by Hervey Allen; "Perpetual Light," by William Rose Benét; "In April Once," by William Alexander Percy; "Along the Wind," by Chard Powers Smith; and "Forgotten Shrines," by John Farrar.

The editor wishes also to thank personally the following poets who have graciously given permission for the use of poems not yet published in book form: Kenneth Slade Alling; Anna Hempstead Branch; John Bennett; Gamaliel Bradford; Gertrude Callaghan; Robert P. Tristram Coffin; Eleanor Rogers Cox; Louise Driscoll; George H. Dillon; Lee Wilson Dodd; Hildegarde Flanner; Agnes Kendrick Gray; Caroline Giltinan; Louis Ginsberg; Herbert Gorman; Frank Ernest

Hill; May Folwell Hoisington; Rolfe Humphries; Leslie
Nelson Jennings; Bernice Lesbia Kenyon; Lawrence Lee;
Ludwig Lewisohn; Don Marquis; Marjorie Meeker; Helene
Mullins; Robert Nathan; Shaemas O'Sheel; William Alex-
ander Percy; Lynn Riggs; Charles Wharton Stork; Constance
Lindsay Skinner; George Brandon Saul; Lilian White Spen-
cer; Marion Strobel; Allen Tate; Virginia Lyne Tunstall;
Mark Turbyfill; Mary Brent Whiteside; Florence Wilkinson;
John V. A. Weaver; Robert Wolf; Charles Erskine Scott
Wood; and Marya Zaturensky.

THE THIRD BOOK
OF MODERN VERSE

TRAGIC BOOKS

THAT I have lived I know; that I
Have loved is quite as plain;
Why read of Lear, a wild old king,
Of Caesar stabbed in vain?

The bitter fool, the Dover heath,
The stumbling in the grass
I know. I know the windy crowd,
And Rome as in a glass.

Life taught them all. These later days
Are full enough of rain;
I will not weep unless I must,
Or break my heart again.

Lizette Woodworth Reese

PASSER MORTUUS EST

DEATH devours all lovely things;
    Lesbia with her sparrow
Shares the darkness — presently
    Every bed is narrow.

Unremembered as old rain
    Dries the sheer libation,
And the little petulant hand
    Is an annotation.

After all, my erstwhile dear,
    My no longer cherished,
Need we say it was not love,
    Now that love is perished?

Edna St. Vincent Millay

3

TO EARTHWARD

LOVE at the lips was touch
As sweet as I could bear;
And once that seemed too much;
I lived on air

That crossed me from sweet things,
The flow of — was it musk
From hidden grapevine springs
Down hill at dusk?

I had the swirl and ache
From sprays of honeysuckle
That when they're gathered shake
Dew on the knuckle.

I craved strong sweets, but those
Seemed strong when I was young;
The petal of the rose
It was that stung.

Now no joy but lacks salt
That is not dashed with pain
And weariness and fault;
I crave the stain

Of tears, the aftermark
Of almost too much love,
The sweet of bitter bark
And burning clove.

When stiff and sore and scarred
I take away my hand
From leaning on it hard
In grass and sand,

The hurt is not enough :
I long for weight and strength
To feel the earth as rough
To all my length.
Robert Frost

HE VISITS A HOSPITAL

Now why should I, who sneer and frown
 With misanthropic hate,
Be, in this horizontal town,
 Swiftly compassionate?

And curiously why should I
 For all my lordly scorn
Shake at the knees to see men die
 Or hear them being born?

My coat of artificial rock
 Externally is firm :
Inside, susceptible of shock,
 And flabby as a worm,

Secretively there lurks, I think,
 The kind of soul that crawls,
For otherwise, why should I shrink
 At entering these walls?
Rolfe Humphries

I CANNOT KNOW THAT OTHER MEN
EXIST

I CANNOT know that other men exist :
 It is but a belief, obscurely guessed.
Upon the mirror, brain, they move in mist ;
 A wall of air holds back the friendliest breast.
To me they are. . . .   And so to me the vision
 My fancy builds this moment in the air,

Food for a clearer glance's high derision,
   Food for a thoughtful hour's thin despair.

For knowledge is from skill of inward seeing,
   Not bred of eye, or ear, or touch, alone:
It is the younger, truer name of being, —
   No gossip spread by careless flesh and bone;
And though from seed to fruit to seed it change,
It is one's self, and knows no further range.

            Clement Wood

THE LION–HOUSE

ALWAYS the heavy air,
   The dreadful cage, the low
Murmur of voices, where
   Some Force goes to and fro
In an immense despair!

As through a haunted brain —
   With tireless footfalls
The Obsession moves again,
   Trying the floor, the walls,
Forever, but in vain.

In vain, proud Force! A might,
   Shrewder than yours, did spin
Around your rage that bright
   Prison of steel, wherein
You pace for my delight.

And O, my heart, what Doom,
   What mightier Will has wrought
The cage, within whose room
   Paces your burning thought,
For the delight of Whom?

          John Hall Wheelock

HAWK SHADOW

That day —
Day was more beautiful than a bitter gem
On the fierce hand you love
Till from above —

That day —
Day was more beautiful than a black goldness in a
     murderous well
Till from the blue there fell —

Than a blood-spotted lily on an acrid stem,
Than black moon in gold water, lily, bitter gem, —
Day was more breathless-beautiful than all of them
Until —

From out the still
Mordant and weaponed sleeping loveliness
Shadow fell.

This way, that way, birch tree shadows go
But hawk shadow, hawk shadow, they who know —
     they know.
This way, that way, south rain shadows float
But hawk shadow, hawk shadow, is hemlock in the
     throat.

Florence Wilkinson

I SAW THAT SHATTERED THING

I saw that shattered thing,
And did not understand
Why to the hovering wing
It raised a tragic hand.

By the accurséd deep
Where the obscure stream flows,
I stood on the black steep,
Uncaring for the woes
That my own spirit knows.

On the abhorrent brink
Where Death is born anew,
And the thinker cannot think,
And the doer cannot do,
There was I too,

Careless and debonnaire
As a child at play,
Nor felt in the black air,
Swirling around me there,
What I must slay —

Achilles with flaming hair
And the unarméd heel,
Balder the fair,
Unpierceable with steel.
They are fallen, slain by craft,
Discrowned of all their light,
By the envenomed shaft,
And the oak's parasite.

Roland's in ill report,
And Charlemagne grows old.
Galahad makes poor sport
For a common whore I'm told.
Lancelot cheats at cards.
Merlin, who rhymes no more,
Has stolen another bard's
Sweet legendary lore.

Gone the enchanted horses,
And the women with wings.
We are on our own resources
With unheroic things.
And that stings.

Uncoils the Midgard Snake;
Atlas lets fall the sky.
What from that night shall wake
When the stars die?
What shall rise from the dark
And the mortal and stricken star?
Life with a perishing spark?
And people that are?

Leonard Bacon

THE TOO–LATE BORN

WE too, we too, descending once again
The hills of our own land, we too have heard
Far off — Ah, que ce cor a longue haleine —
The horn of Roland in the passages of Spain,
The first, the second blast, the failing third,
And with the third turned back and climbed once more
The steep road southward, and heard faint the sound
Of swords, of horses, the disastrous war,
And crossed the dark defile at last, and found
At Ronçevaux upon the darkening plain
The dead against the dead and on the silent ground
The silent slain —

Archibald MacLeish

THE BIRDS

I THOUGHT to shoulder Time but those sad birds
Would speak forever with such fiery words,
Such spinning gusts of warning tenderness
That I was helpless in my nakedness;
And sat down in the desert where the sand
Obliterated years on every hand,
So loath was I to listen.   "See," I said,
"It would be better far if I were dead,
For dead men cannot hear such lovely calls
From bitter birds by Babylonian walls."

And now while chuckling Time still nudges me
Through vague savannahs of immensity,
Speaking in heavy darkness of sharp sighs
Of my befooled and barren enterprise,
And all I was flees in a shadow-show
Of antic shapes in sad imbroglio,
I cry to hear those birds who sing no more
By crumbling wall and splintered palace door,
And search in vain to see those feathered crests
Aflare like jewels in their last year's nests.

Herbert Gorman

THE EAGLE HUNTER

I SAID : I will go down,
    Save me from hurts of height,
    Wounds of renown,
The spurning spears of light
And scorn of the gigantic flight.
    I will desist,
Give up the great antagonist;
    I will go hence

From this most dire magnificence
　　And regal state
　　Of battle desperate;
　　Resign
The hunt of eagles to the fine
And fierce essay, the dare-and-do
Of taller men and new.
　　I will restore
Me to the valley's eve and noon,
And crack my heart no more,
But hide, in poor delight
　　Of harmless things,
From haunt of height
And windy width of wings.

Let fly the towering prey,
Unwieldy as the moon!
I will go down and stay,
Be succored by disgrace,
　　Too mean for high mishap.
Be safe and low my chase,
No Titan in my trap
With conquered terror's mighty eye,
　　And that great sigh
That makes the hunter pale!

Ah, let no sun-insulting sail
Of pinions tempt me now,
　　From my low vow,
Nor giant shapes go by
Between me and the sky!

Rose O'Neill

FOG

INVISIBLE gulls with human voices cry in the sea-cloud,
"There is room, wild minds,
Up high in the cloud; the web and the feather remem-
    ber
Three elements, but here
Is but one, and the webs and the feathers
Subduing but the one
Are the greater, with strength and to spare."
You dream, wild criers,
The peace that all life
Dreams gluttonously, the infinite self that has eaten
Environment, and lives
Alone, unencroached on, perfectly gorged, one God.
Caesar and Napoleon
Visibly acting their dream of that solitude, Christ and
    Gautama,
Being God, devouring
The world with atonement for God's sake . . . ah
    sacred hungers,
The conqueror's, the prophet's,
The lover's, the hunger of the sea-beaks, slaves of the
    last peace,
Worshippers of oneness.

                                    Robinson Jeffers

SONNETS

I

THIRTY-EIGHT years. Yes, neither less nor more,
Of which an anxious third have been spent earning
The pittance of what faute de mieux's called learning.
And two insane, but actual years of war,
And five books written — two out of my heart's core

Full of the fury of my central burning,
Whose heat escapes the reader undiscerning,
Who cannot see what they were written for.

And then for me the cosmos circumspect
Whirling an orrery of lighted gyres,
Steady, superlatively ordered fires,
In one chaotic turmoil crashed together,
Disorbited, annihilated, wrecked.
Can I reshape it?   Well, I wonder whether.

II

Dante was naïf although he had an inkling
Of what I know.   Forgive me if I seem
To boast like one in an ecstatic dream.
I have read a parchment when the leaf was crinkling
In Hell-fire — seen a sacred planet twinkling
The better for the darkness, like the gleam
Of the mystic rose, and heard in my own scream
Cool discrete music, like a Bach fugue tinkling.

I have found at the bottom of all things the height,
The unknown future in the unknown past,
The first of things commingled with the last,
Stability in water, motion in rocks,
Sight in my blindness, blindness in my sight,
And truth perpetual in a paradox.

III

Idiots will prate and prate of suicide.
I shall not take my life.   It has been taken.
They strangled me, and now I lie forsaken
In the cellar of the brothel where I died.
I walk and talk of course.   It's not implied

That this live corpse of mine is never shaken
By startling reflex action.   But what can waken
The slaughtered hope, the immolated pride?

This may appear fantastic.   The fantastic
Is a luxury I cannot now afford.
You, sir, may scatter from your golden horde
Orient conceits.   They cost you but a breath.
But my sad soul was caught in orgiastic
Embraces — and the harlot's name was Death.

Leonard Bacon

TASTING THE EARTH

In a dark hour, tasting the Earth.

As I lay on my couch in the muffled night, and the rain
    lashed my window,
And my forsaken heart would give me no rest, no
    pause and no peace,
Though I turned my face far from the wailing of my
    bereavement,
Then I said: I will eat of this sorrow to its last shred,
I will take it unto me utterly,
I will see if I be not strong enough to contain it.
What do I fear?   Discomfort?
How can it hurt me, this bitterness?

The miracle, then!
Turning toward it, and giving up to it,
I found it deeper than my own self. . . .
O dark great mother-globe so close beneath me!
It was she with her inexhaustible grief,
Ages of blood-drenched jungles, and the smoking of
    craters, and the roar of tempests,

And moan of the forsaken seas.
It was she with the hills beginning to walk in the
    shapes of the dark-hearted animals,
It was she risen, dashing away tears and praying to
    dumb skies, in the pomp-crumbling tragedy
    of man.
It was she, container of all griefs, and the buried dust
    of broken hearts,
Cry of the christs and the lovers and the child-
    stripped mothers,
And ambition gone down to defeat, and the battle
    overborne,
And the dreams that have no waking. . . .

My heart became her ancient heart:
On the food of the strong I fed, on dark strange life
    itself:
Wisdom-giving and sombre with the unremitting love
    of ages. . . .

There was dank soil in my mouth,
And bitter sea on my lips,
In a dark hour, tasting the Earth.

                                James Oppenheim

BIRTH

THE grain of corn within the earth
Knows well the agony of birth:

It lies with stones for bed-fellows
In mould still damp with perished snows;
It feels the dusky, breathless dirt
Heaped on it, and must lie inert
And frigid till the rain-drops swell
(Breaking its heart) its stubborn shell.

Then in slow anguish it must thrust
Its pale head upward through the crust
Of the oblivious earth, and send
Thin fingers of its life to rend
Food from the sunless, deaf, profound,
Stony abysses of the ground.
It has but rain and mould to eat,
And damp pink earthworms at its feet. . . .

So my soul lies, in darker earth,
A seed in agony of birth —
Waiting, half-hopeless, to be born,
Perhaps, as tassel-whispering corn!

E. Merrill Root

VIATICUM

BEAUTY is fashioned out of mud
As well as stars, said Sagramond;
And dark imps dancing in the blood
Throw shadows that extend beyond
This pallid piety of flesh
Groveling in its twisted mesh.

The thing that is, itself becomes
The empty echo of a doubt,
And meaningless as beaten drums
That wheel the vacant mind about
The troubled corridors of noise
Where antic Pantaloon deploys.

Who plucks the burning rose may hold
The sinister embodiment
Of more than petals growing old
And less than man's obscure intent,

For in that crimson dust is fate
And passion transubstantiate.

Who knows the feeble frame of roofs
Upreared against the dark sublime
Where thunder stamps enormous hoofs
Upon the splintered boards of Time?
And who pretends to hide away
From the bright malice of the day?

The shadow that you throw assumes
The majesty that is your mind
And from your self-demolished tombs
You rise up not entirely blind;
Which is, said Sagramond, the sum
Of your desired viaticum.

Herbert Gorman

CONFIDANTS

REJOICE, my heart, that the stars do not comprehend
     you,
That they march on their mighty courses, serene and
     terrible,
Unvexed by your sorrow, untarnished by your desires.
You may spread your pain like a purple cloth before
     them
And their silver and golden feet will brush it lightly
As they brush the cloths of the grass which is more
     beautiful.
You may cry aloud to them your dolor and desolation,
And though your cry were intolerable and keen as
     Israfel's,
They would not heed it, high-hearted in the roar of
     ebbing chaos.

Even your self-pity, shining like a gift and shameless,
You may bring them without evil, for they, they only
    of your comrades,
Resist the infection of sorrow, the contagion of tears.
                    William Alexander Percy

PRAYER FOR PAIN

I DO not pray for peace nor ease,
Nor truce from sorrow :
No suppliant on servile knees
Begs here against to-morrow !

Lean flame against lean flame we flash,
O Fates that meet me fair ;
Blue steel against blue steel we clash —
Lay on, and I shall dare !

But Thou of deeps the awful Deep,
Thou breather in the clay,
Grant this my only prayer — Oh keep
My soul from turning gray !

For until now, whatever wrought
Against my sweet desires,
My days were smitten harps strung taut,
My nights were slumbrous lyres.

And howsoe'er the hard blow rang
Upon my battered shield,
Some lark-like, soaring spirit sang
Above my battle-field ;

And through my soul of stormy night
The zigzag blue flame ran.

I asked no odds — I fought my fight —
Events against a man.

But now — at last — the gray mist chokes
And numbs me. *Leave me pain!*
Oh let me feel the biting strokes
That I may fight again!

John G. Neihardt

GHOSTLY BATTLES

BEFORE the battle soldiers fight the fear
That is in them, and sailors feel the blow
And chill of winds in masts when storm draws near,
And farmers grapple drouth before they sow.
The cactus has its spears before its bloom
And, even near the desert, eagles dwell
In crags where prowling feet may find no room,
And wild geese post their trusted sentinel.

These are the ghostly battles of the will
In which we may not know the thing we fight
Save as a force to thwart and mar and kill
And hold us back from some inherent right
That gives a sense of ghostly banners blown
In victories that are not all our own.

Glenn Ward Dresbach

SLEEPERS

HERE are the tiny lads, the grave, the dream-lit faces,
With sad Shakespearean smiles, and glad Catullan
    graces.

Tonight the moon guards some weird window-pane,
Where Abel sleeps again with jealous Cain.

Behind a dusty lintel doubtless lies
A tired cherub, with dead Dante's eyes.

For whoso tells how cryptic years conspire
To build a saint's white heart, a bandit's ire?

Along a street, mantled in bitter snows,
A young Napoleon sleeps — who knows, who knows?

And Paganini peeps again from bed,
To hear the lark's first song when dawn is red.

Madman, murderer, priest, they all sleep well,
For what the years shall make them, none can tell.

The little lads — the grave, the dream-lit faces,
With sad Shakespearean eyes, and glad Catullan
  graces.
       J. Corson Miller

BLESSING ON LITTLE BOYS

God bless all little boys who look like Puck,
 With wide eyes, wider mouths and stick-out ears,
Rash little boys who stay alive by luck
 And Heaven's favor in this world of tears,
Ten-thousand-question-asking little boys,
 Rapid of hand and foot and thought as well,
Playing with gorgeous fancies more than toys,
 Heroes of what they dream, but never tell;
Father, in your vast playground let them know
 The loveliness of ocean, star and hill;
Protect from every bitterness and woe
 Your heedless little acolytes, and still
Grant me the grace, I beg upon my knees,
Not to forget that I was one of these.
       Arthur Guiterman

THE SCHOOL-BOY READS HIS ILIAD

THE sounding battles leave him nodding still :
   The din of javelins at the distant wall
Is far too faint to wake that weary will
   That all but sleeps for cities where they fall.
He cares not if this Helen's face were fair,
   Nor if the thousand ships shall go or stay ;
In vain the rumbling chariots throng the air
   With sounds the centuries shall not hush away.

Beyond the window where the Spring is new,
   Are marbles in a square, and tops again,
And floating voices tell him what they do,
   Luring his thought from these long-warring men, —
And though the camp be visited with gods,
He dreams of marbles and of tops, and nods.
                     David Morton

BOY IN THE WIND

How came this troubled one to stray
With fire and song in the wind's way ?

Indifferent and dumb and sweet,
The seasons fall about his feet.

Frail flames are set behind his eyes,
And under his ribs his heart makes moan
Like a pent bird who throbs and dies.

He walks in the windy night alone.

And who would know if he should sing
Whose song is less than the murmuring
Of the wind full of the ruin of spring ?

And who could say if he had flown
Like a flame blown out or a bird upblown?

Or if his heart cries out in pain
Who hears the cry through wind and rain?

He wanders east.   He wanders west.

Where will he ever come to rest
With that fire blowing in his brain
And that bird grieving in his breast?

George H. Dillon

WISDOM COMETH WITH THE YEARS

Now I am young and credulous,
  My heart is quick to bleed
At courage in the tremulous
  Slow sprouting of a seed.

Now I am young and sensitive,
  Man's lack can stab me through;
I own no stitch I would not give
  To him that asked me to.

Now I am young and a fool for love,
  My blood goes mad to see
A brown girl pass me like a dove
  That flies melodiously.

Let me be lavish of my tears
  And dream that false is true;
Though wisdom cometh with the years,
  The barren days come, too.

Countee Cullen

TO YOUTH

THIS I say to you:
Be arrogant! Be true!
True to April lust that sings
Through your veins. These sharp springs
Matter most. . . . Afteryears
Will be time enough for sleep . . .
Carefulness . . . and tears. . . .

Now, while life is raw and new,
Drink it clear, drink it deep!
Let the moonlight's lunacy
Tear away your cautions. Be
Proud, and mad, and young, and free!
Grasp a comet! Kick at stars
Laughingly! Fight! Dare!
Arms are soft, breasts are white,
Magic's in the April night —

Never fear, Age will catch you,
Slow you down, ere it dispatch you
To your long and solemn quiet. . . .

What will matter then the riot
Of the lilacs in the wind?
What will mean — then — the crush
Of lips at hours when birds hush?

Purple, green and flame will end
In a calm, grey blend.

Only . . . graven in your soul
After all the rest is gone
There will be the ecstasies . . .
Those alone. . . .

John V. A. Weaver

ADVICE TO A YOUNG ROMANTICIST

Young man, you hold your head
Too high in the air, you walk
As if the sleepy dead
Had never fallen to drowse
From the sublimest talk
Of many a vehement house.
Your head, so turned, turns eyes
Following a vagrant West;
Fixing an iron mood
In an Ozymandias' breast,
And because your clamorous blood
Beats an impermanent rest
You think the dead arise
Westward and fabulous:
The dead are those whose lies
Were doors to a narrow house.

Allen Tate

CONFESSION

I think, by God! It is no lie;
I shall go dreaming till I die!
There is no love so real to me
As the cold passion of the sea.
There is no little, wind-swept town
By harbors where the roads go down,
Or headland gray that sits and sips
The cup of ocean at its lips,
And gazes at the far-off ships —
Or tree or house or friend so real
As visions and the dreams I feel.

No — not the windy, vaultless arch
Where all the white stars flame and march,

Nor water at the river fords
Like horses mad among the swords,
Or oaks that lean from winter storms;
These only give my vision forms.

Away! White hands, I will not take!
And kissing mouths that cry, "Awake!"
For you I have no gramercy;
So leave me by my lotus tree,
To dream and gaze into the sky
Where red suns wither up and die,
I know! I know! I do not lie!
I shall go dreaming till I die!

Hervey Allen

PRAYER AFTER YOUTH

O GODS of all enchanting lies,
Hear now the louder voice that cries
Forever in me, crying and rising,
That I am lost beyond devising
Of the fearful blood or the quick brain
Here puzzling in the dark in vain
How I may live, how I may not die
While the bright days fall silently
And one by one through a cold heaven
The bright years fall that I am given
Out of silence and out of sound
Before I turn me back to ground.

O falling of water, passing of wind,
Hear this now — the blood is thinned,
The blue broods lower, the night clings
All day long to the cumbered wings,

And late or soon but sooner now
The singing grass and the singing bough
Where my eternal summer was
I shall not find in tree or grass.
No, though the flickering dancers run
Endless ever through shadow and sun
And laughter slips along the dusk
And lover on lover turns to ask
What was given before words were,
Though wine be dark and lips be myrrh
And I still live and look on this
I shall be hollow as emptiness,
And the shadows before my eyes
Will be shadows of memories.

O mist of rivers running with death,
Hear this now, this is my breath
Crying forever, crying in fear
Of the eternal messenger
Whispering to me in a near night:
Oh, now look backward to delight;
Whispering, in the brain's chamber —
What was yours you may remember,
Still the long bolt of your weaving
May unroll for your deceiving,
But the years' meridian
Passes and comes not again,
And ever lower the pole-star
Rides behind the mariner.
Oh, all gods of enchanting lies,
Hear now the louder voice that cries
Forever in me, crying and rising,
That I am lost beyond devising. . . .

                              Maxwell Anderson

COMPOSITION

"To sleep: perchance to dream. . . ." He turned
    his head
And saw day's flare behind the heavy tower.
"Ay, there's the rub; for in that sleep" — he said,
And stared into the river for an hour.

"The pangs of disprized love. . . ." He frowned
    and shifted.
Fog crept upon the unawakened town;
Out on the muddy flow a dark swan drifted
And far along the shore vague bells came down.

"The undiscovered country. . . ." There he turned
And heard a woman weeping in the street,
And saw a window where a candle burned
And caught the echo of departing feet.

"Thus conscience does make cowards. . . ." Morn-
    ing drew
Pale silver to the marsh through willow stems.
He scraped the edges of a muddy shoe
And spat into the Thames.

George O'Neil

L'AN TRENTIESME DE MON EAGE

AND I have come upon this place
By lost ways, by a nod, by words,
By faces, by an old man's face
At Morlaix lifted to the birds,

By hands upon the tablecloth
At Aldebori's, by the thin

Child's hands that opened to the moth
And let the flutter of the moonlight in,

By hands, by voices, by the voice
Of Mrs. Husman on the stair,
By Margaret's "If we had the choice
To choose or not" — through her thick hair,

By voices, by the creak and fall
Of footsteps on the upper floor,
By silence waiting in the hall
Between the doorbell and the door,

By words, by voices, a lost way —
And here above the chimney stack
The unknown constellations sway —
And by what way shall I go back?

Archibald MacLeish

PITY

I DO not pity the old men, fumbling after
The golden bird of love, the purple grapes of laughter;
They drank honey once, they fingered the falcon's hood.
I do not pity the old, with ash in their veins for blood.
It is the young whom I pity, the young who are lovely
    and cruel,
The young whose lips and limbs are time's quick-col-
    ored fuel.
Death can comfort the old; pain, age understands —
Not the tossed bright head of folly, the soft impatient
    hands.
I do not pity the old men's forgetful tears and mirth.
But the young must eat pomegranate seeds in the
    darkness under the earth.

Babette Deutch

LET ME LIVE OUT MY YEARS

LET me live out my years in heat of blood!
Let me die drunken with the dreamer's wine!
Let me not see this soul-house built of mud
Go toppling to the dust — a vacant shrine.

Let me go quickly, like a candle light
Snuffed out just at the heyday of its glow.
Give me high noon — and let it then be night!
Thus would I go.

And grant that when I face the grisly Thing,
My song may trumpet down the grey Perhaps.
O let me be a tune-swept fiddle string
That feels the Master-Melody — and snaps!

John G. Neihardt

FOR A POET GROWING OLD

IF you should go, and beauty still be hidden
Beyond the woods and the last meadow wall,
We shall keep up the lonely chase, unbidden,
Except by a far horn which we heard call.
Who catches beauty as a hound must run,
Nose in the wind and trembling for the race;
And we, whose hunt is scarcely well begun,
Feel, with the thrill, the terror of the chase.
Yet, should our eager muzzles never find
The fields where beauty in her speed goes by,
Or we, grown old, come limping up the wind,
There shall be younger hounds to hear the cry
And leap to overtake her like a hind;
And down the world the hunt shall never die.

Lawrence Lee

MAY UPON ICTIS

FAR out at sea beneath rich Tyrian sails
  The merchants watch a ghostly mountain spread
  Terrific dawn-wings fired with cloudy red,
And cease their barter over purple bales;
Wild headland flames to headland; in the dales
  Hushed warriors wait, for no torqued chief may
      tread
  That dim white forest where the vanished dead
Gather like birds before the spume-drenched gales.

Around the mount barbaric trumpets cry;
  Then Ictis thunders through her altar-stone,
    Long cloven by a god's mysterious rune;
And pinnacled between the earth and sky
  Her savage prophet stands, majestic, lone,
    Helmed with the sun and girdled with the moon.
                              Thomas S. Jones, Jr.

VOYAGES

WHERE icy and bright dungeons lift
Of swimmers their lost morning eyes,
And ocean rivers, churning, shift
Green borders under stranger skies,

Steadily as a shell secretes
Its beating leagues of monotone,
Or as many waters trough the sun's
Red kelson past the cape's wet stone;

O rivers mingling toward the sky
And harbor of the phœnix' breast —
My eyes pressed black against the prow,
— Thy derelict and blinded guest

Waiting, afire, what name, unspoke,
I cannot claim: let thy waves rear
More savage than the death of kings,
Some splintered garland for the seer.

Beyond siroccos harvesting
The solstice thunders, crept away,
Like a cliff swinging or a sail
Flung into April's inmost day —

Creation's blithe and petalled word
To the lounged goddess when she rose
Conceding dialogue with eyes
That smile unsearchable repose —

Still fervid covenant, Belle Isle,
— Unfolded floating dais before
Which rainbows twine continual hair —
Belle Isle, white echo of the oar!

The imaged Word, it is, that holds
Hushed willows anchored in its glow.
It is the unbetrayable reply
Whose accent no farewell can know.

Hart Crane

THE ISLANDS

I

WHAT are the islands to me,
what is Greece,
what is Rhodes, Samos, Chios,
what is Paros facing west,
what is Crete?

What is Samothrace,
rising like a ship,
what is Imbros rending the storm-waves
with its breast?

What is Naxos, Paros, Milos,
what the circle about Lycia,
what the Cyclades'
white necklace?

What is Greece —
Sparta, rising like a rock,
Thebes, Athens,
What is Corinth?

What is Euboia
with its island violets,
what is Euboia, spread with grass,
set with swift shoals,
what is Crete?

What are the islands to me,
what is Greece?

II

What can love of land give to me
that you have not —
what do the tall Spartans know,
and gentler Attic folk?

What has Sparta and her women
more than this?

What are the islands to me
If you are lost —

what is Naxos, Tinos, Andros,
and Delos, the clasp
of the white necklace?

III

What can love of land give to me
that you have not,
what can love of strife break in me
that you have not?

Though Sparta enter Athens,
Thebes wreck Sparta,
each changes as water,
salt, rising to wreak terror
and fall back.

IV

"What has love of land given to you
that I have not?"

I have questioned Tyrians
where they sat
on the black ships,
weighted with rich stuffs,
I have asked the Greeks
from the white ships,
and Greeks from ships whose hulks
lay on the wet sand, scarlet
with great beaks.
I have asked bright Tyrians
and tall Greeks —
"What has love of land given you?"
And they answered — "peace."

V

But beauty is set apart,
beauty is cast by the sea,
a barren rock,
beauty is set about
with wrecks of ships,
upon our coast, death keeps
the shallows — death waits
clutching toward us
from the deeps.

Beauty is set apart;
the winds that slash its beach,
swirl the coarse sand
upward toward the rocks.
Beauty is set apart
from the islands
and from Greece.

VI

In my garden
the winds have beaten
the ripe lilies;
In my garden, the salt
has wilted the first flakes
of young narcissus,
and the lesser hyacinth,
and the salt has crept
under the leaves of the white hyacinth.

In my garden
even the wind-flowers lie flat,
broken by the wind at last.

VII

What are the islands to me
if you are lost,
what is Paros to me
if your eyes draw back,
what is Milos
if you take fright of beauty,
terrible, torturous, isolated,
a barren rock?

What is Rhodes, Crete,
what is Paros facing west,
what, white Imbros?

What are the islands to me
if you hesitate,
what is Greece if you draw back
from the terror
and cold splendour of song
and its bleak sacrifice?

H. D.

THE GREATER MYSTERY

WE journey to Eleusis, you and I,
  And walk the curving road beside the sea,
  Both pilgrims to the Greater Mystery,
And seekers for the truth before we die;
We who have asked of all earth's wisest why,
  And entered every temple eagerly,
  Accosters of each high philosophy,
Now yield the futile question with a sigh.
That sapphire is the wave of Salamis,
  Those bees are from Hymettus, and the breath
  Of Attic summer brings abiding bliss;

So Nature turns us from the thought of death,
And we submissive, at the darkened door,
   Accept her mood and question her no more.
                  John Myers O'Hara

BITTER BREAD AND WEAK WINE

I HAVE tasted Sorrow,
I have eaten her whole,
And her bitter marrow
Has fed my sick soul.

With hunger abated,
Desireless I sup,
And drink unelated
From Joy's tilted cup.

Can such listless quaffing
From waters so mild,
Restore me to laughing
And the faith of a child?
                  Jean Starr Untermeyer

CURE–ALL

TELL me, is there sovereign cure
   For heart-ache, heart-ache, —
Cordial quick and potion sure
   For heart-ache, heart-ache?

Fret thou not. If all else fail
   For heart-ache, heart-ache,
One thing surely will avail, —
   That's heart-break, heart-break!
                  Edith M. Thomas

FLOWERS OF APOLLO

The flowers of Apollo that will heal
Are laid across my anger and my eyes.
Oh, once-belovèd, where they set their seal,
I have grown merry and I shall grow wise.
But lest my merriment should flutter out
And wisdom fall in shadows and in night,
I must forget what I grow wise about,
And why I laugh must be forgotten quite.
And so my memory on whispering feet
Goes nowhere in a dim processional,
While I (with Lenten eyes) along the street
Come homeward from a dumb confessional.
I will not tell how many times I break
The flowers of Apollo for your sake.

Hildegarde Flanner

MY SONG

My song that was a sword is still.
Like a scabbard I have made
A covering with my will
To sheathe its blade.

It had a flashing tongue of steel
That made old shadows start;
It would not let the darkness heal
About my heart.

Hazel Hall

MY DARKNESS

Oh come, my darkness!
There has been too much of light,
Too much of heaping noon.
Give me the empty night!

And let there be
No ministration of the moon,
Nor gold along the sea.

Let no leaf
Turn argent, and no tree
Be quickened into silver grief:
Fold up the arduous bright;
Beat down and still
The howling of the kennelled will
And hungry hounds of sight!
Oh come, my darkness!

Rose O'Neill

REVISITANTS

WE who went where Dante went,
  And Persephone,
You can know us by the bent
  Brow, and shadowy;

By the eyes that still would dream
  (Through your loudest word)
Of the kindness in some stream
  And some singing bird.

Soft our words to all who live,
  Courteously we go
(There's so little to forgive,
  Knowing what we know!)

Yet have patience if we stare
  At your whimpering crowd. . . .
Where the Nine Great Circles were
  No man cried aloud.

Margaret Widdemer

FORGIVENESS

Now God be thanked that roads are long and wide,
  And four far havens in the scattered sky :
  It would be hard to meet and pass you by.

And God be praised there is an end of pride,
  And pity only has a word to say,
  While memory grows dim as time grows gray.

For, God His word, I gave my best to you,
  All that I had, the finer and the sweet,
  To make — a path for your unquiet feet.

Their track is on the life they trampled through;
  Such evil steps to leave such hallowing.
  Now God be with them in their wandering.
                                    Charles L. O'Donnell

COMRADE TO COMRADE

Comrade to comrade we shall talk at last
When unemcumbered by our temporal clay
We watch the archangelic whirlwinds play
Above the worlds, as once above the vast
Of chaos blew the Holy Breath, and fast,
Faster than any thought of ours may say,
Our words will pierce eternal night and day
When God has given the future to the past.

And we shall talk knowing as we are known
In the bright placid mirror of His look,
Never bewildered, nevermore alone
When He has given more than ever He took
And all His loveliest mysteries are shown
As open legends in an ancient book.
                                    Marguerite Wilkinson

I AM UNDONE

I COULD bear grief, if it were only thorough,
  If it were sharp and brief,
And measured to my strongest mesh of armor.
  I could bear grief.

But sadness like the pressure of a snowfall
  Upon a fall of snow,
Because it seems unworthy of my rapier,
  Too slight a foe,

Betrays me as I sit and sing at evening
  For happiness half won:
I am undone by sifting, snowflake sadness;
  I am undone.

Virginia Moore

PAGEANT

THOUGH I go by with banners,
  Oh, never envy me
These flags of scarlet flying,
  This purple that you see. . . .

This air of marching triumph
  Was all that I could save
Of loves that had an ending
  And hopes that had a grave.

Margaret Widdemer

NEVER HURT THE PROUD

NEVER hurt the proud
Lest the wound stay
Long ages through
Like a mark in clay

Till the soul is old,
Till the clay is stone,
And till love is gone.

Speak against the wind,
Or on humble sand
Write the cruel word;
Waves will understand.
Swiftly they will come
To wash the spirit clean
Of mad thought and mean.

Never hurt the proud,
For not every pride
Is so firm in power
That it can deride
Even its own wound.
Oh, let love alone
Be graven on the stone.

Marguerite Wilkinson

YOUR TEARS

I DARE not ask your very all:
  I only ask a part.
Bring me — when dancers leave the hall —
  Your aching heart.

Give other friends your lighted face,
  The laughter of the years:
I come to crave a greater grace —
  Bring me your tears!

Edwin Markham

THE PUPIL RETURNS TO HIS MASTER

It is because they troubled me
I am come back to you.
They would not leave my eyelids free
To stare at the noon's high blue.

They would not let my ears escape
Their clack and clamoring.
They would not let my dreams take shape
To one clear lovely thing.

They talked to me, and talked to me,
And sat up close, and stared.
I would have cast them in the sea,
Or choked them, had I dared.

But they were kind; and hurting seems
A childish hatefulness. . . .
All that I need now are my dreams,
Quiet and comradeless. . . .

Oh, I will work my hands to bone,
And sew my lids with thorns,
For you, who leave me all alone
As the moon's polished horns!

Oh, I will serve you like a slave, —
Because you know that I
Must keep alone, alone, to save
The soul you taught to fly!

Fannie Stearns Davis

ESCAPE

WHEN foxes eat the last gold grape,
And the last white antelope is killed,
I shall stop fighting and escape
Into a little house I'll build.

But first I'll shrink to fairy size,
With a whisper no one understands,
Making blind moons of all your eyes,
And muddy roads of all your hands.

And you may grope for me in vain
In hollows under the mangrove root,
Or where, in apple-scented rain,
The silver wasp-nests hang like fruit.

Elinor Wylie

THE BLACK ROSE

THERE is none
Under sun
Like to her.

Where her crowned
Tresses stir,
Death has found
Sepulchre.

Every leaf
Black with grief:
And her scent
Is torment.

She is cold
As the old

Shrunken moon
At blue noon:
As a sped
Wind from Hell:
As a dead
Miracle.

Yet she lifts
One by one,
Petals dead,
Black, and old,
To the sun —
And his gold
Slowly drifts
Round her head —
A divine
Seal and sign.

And the suns,
Singing ones,
Are all bowed
At her feet
In a sweet
Fiery cloud.

Where her crowned
Tresses stir,
Now they sound,
Greeting her —
Dulcimer,
Icy flute,
Mellow lute,
And a lyre
Breathing fire. . . .

Yet the gong
Mutes its song;
Horns of steel
Dim their peal:
Trumpets kneel.

Every leaf
Sheds its grief;
And her scent
Sacrament,
Breathing myrrh.

There is none
Under sun
Like to her.

Clement Wood

UNDEDICATED

THE very sounding of her name
Contracts my throat like searing flame,
My heart beats heavy and too strong
As hidden tears exalt her song,
Her mind unchained, her racing blood
That lifts a lyric like a flood.
Gold trumpet she, but shoulder-flung,
And put to lip, or thrown to dung
By any lad whose vanity
Hears in her lovely note his cry . . .
But I'm a steel held scabbard-straight
And tempered long against my fate.
Oh, she may be the Horn of the Lord
But I will be his Sword — his Sword!

Jean Starr Untermeyer

BETRAYED

SHE is false, O Death, she is fair!
  Let me hide my head on thy knee;
Blind mine eyes, dull mine ears, O Death!
  She hath broken my heart for me!

Give me a perfect dream;
  Find me a rare, dim place;
But let not her voice come nigh,
  And keep out her face — her face!
Lizette Woodworth Reese

LOVE HATH NO PHYSIC FOR A GRIEF
TOO DEEP

Love hath no physic for a grief too deep,
But like the adder that with poisoned breath
Bites its own wound and stings itself to sleep,
So with its hurt love wounds itself to death.
That slender serpent, mottled as the pest,
Is its own merciful and bitter friend;
Hast thou a grief? Go clasp it to thy breast;
Hast thou a poison? Drain it to the end.
Cry, then, cry all thy heart out with its pain;
Hearts grow again, and eyes have better sight
After too many tears, as summer rain
Washes the air and leaves it sweet and bright;
And birds step out on trees, whose happy song
Is often stilled, but never stilled for long.
Robert Nathan

ALADDIN AND THE JINN

"BRING me soft song," said Aladdin.
"This tailor-shop sings not at all.
Chant me a word of the twilight,
Of roses that mourn in the fall.
Bring me a song like hashish
That will comfort the stale and the sad,
For I would be mending my spirit,
Forgetting these days that are bad,
Forgetting companions too shallow,
Their quarrels and arguments thin,
Forgetting the shouting Muezzin;" —
"*I am your slave,*" said the Jinn.

"Bring me old wines," said Aladdin.
"I have been a starved pauper too long.
Serve them in vessels of jade and of shell,
Serve them with fruit and with song: —
Wines of pre-Adamite Sultans
Digged from beneath the black seas: —
New-gathered dew from the heavens
Dripped down from Heaven's sweet trees,
Cups from the angels' pale tables
That will make me both handsome and wise,
For I have beheld her, the princess,
Firelight and starlight her eyes.
Pauper I am, I would woo her.
And — let me drink wine, to begin,
Though the Koran expressly forbids it."
"*I am your slave,*" said the Jinn.

"Plan me a dome," said Aladdin,
"That is drawn like the dawn of the moon,

When the sphere seems to rest on the mountains,
Half-hidden, yet full-risen soon."
"Build me a dome," said Aladdin,
"That shall cause all young lovers to sigh,
The fullness of life and of beauty,
Peace beyond peace to the eye —
A palace of foam and of opal,
Pure moonlight without and within,
Where I may enthrone my sweet lady."
"*I am your slave*," said the Jinn.

Vachel Lindsay

APOLOGY

I AM a poetaster
　And my knee I bend
To Marlowe, my master,
　Villon, my friend.

I am a swashbuckler,
　And I break my sword
Before Blake, my tutor,
　Shakespeare, my lord.

I should burn my song-books
　This very day
If singing didn't matter
　So little anyway.

John McClure

UTTERANCE

I AM not what my lips explain,
But more devotedly inclined
Than these dry sentences reveal
That break in crude shards from my mind.

What way is there of gesturing
The cruelly impounded thought?
It comes, it pierces me like steel,
It flames, but I can utter naught.

The soul so struggling to upheave
Its changeful self, the wistful me,
Is caught in labyrinthean ways
And tangled irrevocably.

And am I worth the guess you make?
O fact so digged in circumstance!
It surely is not known to me,
And you must take my Self on chance.

Donald Davidson

REPLYING TO THE MANY KIND FRIENDS WHO ASK ME IF I NO LONGER WRITE POETRY

Music is writ by the deaf
and poems by the blind.
The sage who utters wisdom
has little on the mind.
Before I had to use them
to find my way about,
Mine eyes would let in Beauty
and shut Time out.
When I was able
to keep the world hid,
Beauty would nestle
under each lid.
When I heard nothing
there echoed in my ears
Certain cadenzas

from the Song of the Spheres.
And in a mind
sinless of thought,
Fragments of wisdom
casually caught.

Now, what would you?
Mind, ears and eyes
guard me like sentinels
and serve me like spies.
They must be wide open
to see and to hear
All that is obvious,
all that is near,
And to think shrewd thoughts
with logic and reason,
And know what the time is
and what's the season.

So while I think
and see and hear
And hold my soul taut
to grapple Fear,
The leering tyrant
of the world I live in,
Swift to crush me
if I give in,
Beauty cannot come
stealing from behind,
Nor fragments of wisdom
catch in the mind.
The best I can do
is now and then to fashion
Some measured thought

with guarded passion.
But till I'm blind again
and deaf, I assure you,
I'll write no poems
to lift and allure you.

Shaemas O'Sheel

THE HARPER

BECAUSE of one whose footstep never fell
In any house of his, he made his songs.
Because of one that had no thing to tell
To him, he sang of beauty that belongs
Only to women dwelling far away
In that enchanted land of Heart's Desire.
Brooding on one that whispered and was gay
Beneath the stars or by an open fire,
And he not there, he learned so much of pain
That madness came upon him, and he ran,
Calling on death down every lonely lane.
He was a foolish and unhappy man
Before he was a poet.   Let there be
None to envy him now that has the praise
Of men upon him, and their courtesy.
Wisdom came to him after nights and days
Of wandering in the dark, and I am thinking
There's none would want his pain or want at all
His lonely hours of making songs and sinking
Wearily down against a ruined wall
After each song is done, and never knowing,
In his eternal brooding, if the hands
That raise him are for healing, or bestowing
Upon his soul the chill of shadowy lands.

Helene Mullins

A MAN BESMITTEN SO

THERE never was a man besmitten so
With self, he couldn't throw the thing aside
If drifting clouds but sued him forth to ride
The undulating waters of the blue —
To leave the self behind or let it blow
Off to the yesterdays that never glide
The same sky twice, nor ever could abide
That they toward other days should onward flow —

Except a man I know of conscious parts,
Who sits him down from dawn to dusk to dark
To squander each and every, all the arts
Toward urging fourteen lines to be a lark ! —
Who thinks, if thoughts grow words, and words a
        throng,
The sum of such a noise would sing a song !
                                        Alfred Kreymborg

I ALMOST HAD FORGOTTEN

I ALMOST had forgotten
    What lonely midnight meant —
The sky too sweet for sleeping,
    With speckle-stars besprent.

I almost had forgotten
    The old sweet folly: how
I sat with ink, outwatching
    Orion and the Plough.

I almost had forgotten
    That love is dearth and pain,
And how the body's vigil
    Is goaded by the brain.

I almost had forgotten
    That words were made for rhyme:
And yet how well I knew it —
    Once upon a time!
Christopher Morley

THE FLOWER

OUR songs are dead, and dead in vain;
To-morrow's song is yet to sing:
Old grayness of the earthy brain,
Out of your dearth what blossoming?

It will not come for waiting long,
For asking much it will not be.
No mendicant has snatched a song
From the close palm of Poesy.

She passes, pale with scorn; her eyes
Are cold to wretchedness, her ears
Deaf to all whining. Nor none buys
Her folded ballads, it appears.

She passes, silent. The years pass.
Comes then a month, a day, an hour,
And to some unexpected lass,
Some gangling lad, she flings — *the Flower*.
Lee Wilson Dodd

PRELUDE

PONDER the tone; the broken theme
Sounds once for us, and not for long.
It is easy to forget a dream,
However exquisite it seem;
It is easy to forget a song.

The Master does but improvise,
The final music is not yet;
But when it shakes eternal skies
I would not have you quite forget
The music of the mortal dream
We shared in joy, though not for long.
Ponder the tone, the broken theme,
It is easy to forget a song.

Robert Hillyer

TOO MANY SONGS

Too many pretty songs are sung —
There is no sinew left in speech,
No burly splendor of the tongue
With power to grip or reach!

Words that were giants long ago
Are bred to-day of poorer bone.
They cannot lift my heart although
They strain forever at the stone.

Amanda Benjamin Hall

ARS POETICA

A POEM should be palpable and mute
As a globed fruit

Dumb
As old medallions to the thumb

Silent as the sleeve-worn stone
Of casement ledges where the moss has grown —

A poem should be wordless
As the flight of birds

A poem should be motionless in time
As the moon climbs

Leaving, as the moon releases
Twig by twig the night entangled trees,

Leaving, as the moon behind the winter leaves,
Memory by memory the mind —

A poem should be motionless in time
As the moon climbs

*   *   *

A poem should be equal to:
Not true

For all the history of grief
An empty doorway and a maple leaf

For love
The leaning grasses and two lights above the sea —

A poem should not mean
But be.

Archibald MacLeish

WORDS

WORDS with the freesia's wounded scent I know
    And those that suck the slow, irresolute gold
    Out of the daffodil's heart; cool words that hold
The crushed gray light of rain, or liquidly blow
The wild bee droning home across the glow
    Of rippled wind-silver; or, uncontrolled,
    Toss the bruised aroma of pine; and words as cold
As water torturing through frozen snow.

And there are words that strain like April hedges
  Upward, lonely words with tears on them;
And syllables whose haunting crimson edges
  Bleed: "O Jerusalem, Jerusalem!"
And that long star-drift of bright agony:
  "Eli, Eli, lama sabachthani!"

Joseph Auslander

MANY ARE CALLED

THE Lord Apollo, who has never died,
Still holds alone his immemorial reign,
Supreme in an impregnable domain
That with his magic he has fortified;
And though melodious multitudes have tried
In ecstasy, in anguish, and in vain,
With invocation sacred and profane
To lure him, even the loudest are outside.

Only at unconjectured intervals,
By will of him on whom no man may gaze,
By word of him whose law no man has read,
A questing light may rift the sullen walls,
To cling where mostly its infrequent rays
Fall golden on the patience of the dead.

Edwin Arlington Robinson

TO E. A. R.

CENTURIES shall not deflect
Nor many suns
Absorb your stream,
Flowing immune and cold
Between the banks of snow.
Nor any wind

Carry the dust of cities
To your high waters
That arise out of the peaks
And return again into the mountains
And never descend.

Lola Ridge

TO THE STONE–CUTTERS

STONE-CUTTERS fighting time with marble, you fore-
    defeated
Challengers of oblivion
Eat cynical earnings, knowing rock splits, records fall
    down,
The square-limbed Roman letters
Scale in the thaws, wear in the rain.   The poet as well
Builds his monument mockingly;
For man will be blotted out, the blithe earth die, the
    brave sun
Die blind, his heart blackening:
Yet stones have stood for a thousand years, and pained
    thoughts found
The honey peace in old poems.

Robinson Jeffers

TO RODIN

On seeing one of his statues in a group of Grecian masterpieces

SMOOTH-BROWED they stand, these marble forms of
    old,
Olympianly serene, without a trace
Of all the throes that won their tranquil grace;
They view mankind with looks aloof and cold.

For though their glorious limbs retain the mould
Of mortal beauty, they admit no place
To struggling imperfection, — every face
A snow-pure height that cloudless beams enfold.

Not so, brave master, was your vision wrought.
That glance of blinded ecstasy has known
The spasms of despair; that breast, still caught
In swathes of rock, still breathes a mighty groan.
There throbs the beauty of a poet's thought
That strains toward God through clinging veils of
      stone.

                    Charles Wharton Stork

ANSWER

I DEMANDED beauty, tasking
Heaven with my asking:
I dared command
Lords of a greater land.
I, who could petition so,
How little did I know!
Fast on beauty's name
Came this blinding flame . . .
Such prayers are always granted, —
But beauty was not what I wanted;
(*I, that asked to sing,*
Sought not this shattering thing . . .)
Not for searing fire
Was my small desire;
You that pray to unknown lords,
Guard your words!

                    Isabel Fiske Conant

EUCLID ALONE HAS LOOKED ON BEAUTY BARE

EUCLID alone has looked on Beauty bare.
Let all who prate of Beauty hold their peace,
And lay them prone upon the earth and cease
To ponder on themselves, the while they stare
At nothing, intricately drawn nowhere
In shapes of shifting lineage; let geese
Gabble and hiss, but heroes seek release
From dusty bondage into luminous air.
O blinding hour, O holy, terrible day,
When first the shaft into his vision shone
Of light anatomized! Euclid alone
Has looked on Beauty bare.   Fortunate they
Who, though once only and then but far away,
Have heard her massive sandal set on stone.

Edna St. Vincent Millay

THE SPRING

CYDONIAN Spring with her attendant train,
Maelids and water-girls,
Stepping beneath a boisterous wind from Thrace,
Throughout this sylvan place
Spreads the bright tips,
And every vine-stock is
Clad in new brilliances.

And wild desire

Falls like black lightning.
O bewildered heart,
Though every branch have back what last year lost,
She, who moved here amid the cyclamen,
Moves only now a clinging tenuous ghost.

Ezra Pound

WILD PLUM

THEY are unholy who are born
   To love wild plum at night,
Who once have passed it on a road
   Glimmering and white.

It is as though the darkness had
   Speech of silver words,
Or as though a cloud of stars
   Perched like ghostly birds.

They are unpitied from their birth
   And homeless in men's sight
Who love better than the earth
   Wild plum at night.

Orrick Johns

WILD CHERRY

BRANCHES of wild cherry!
My senses reeling on the honey-sweet odour.
Brief Spring, brief love, and again
Branches of wild cherry;
Spring succeeding spring
But not love again.

Life, you are a poor barterer.
You give a whole year for a handful of white petals,
Four seasons for one honey-sweet bough —
A branch of wild cherry
Swept bare by the first wind.
You give many years — a lifetime —
For a few kisses, a few broken words.

Jeanne Robert Foster

WHEN TROUT SWIM DOWN GREAT ORMOND STREET

WHEN trout swim down Great Ormond Street
And sea-gulls cry above them lightly
And hawthorns heave cold flagstones up
To blossom whitely

Against old walls of houses there,
Gustily shaking out in moonlight
Their country sweetness on sweet air;
And in the sunlight

By the green margin of that water
Children dip white feet and shout,
Casting nets in the braided water
To catch the trout:

Then I shall hold my breath and die,
Swearing I never loved you; no,
'You were not lovely!' I shall cry,
'I never loved you so.'

Conrad Aiken

RECUERDO

IN Ponce I remembered
The slow curve of the sea.
I saw your ship through flowers
Of the flamboyant tree.

I saw your eyes in shadow
Morning could not erase,
I thought of you in Ponce,
That sun-bewildered place;

Knowing that you would want me
Always a little less,
I warned my heart against you
With no bitterness.

Grace Hazard Conkling

PARADOX

I WENT out to the woods to-day
   To hide away from you,
From you a thousand miles away —
   But you came, too.

And yet the old dull thought would stay
   And all my heart benumb —
If you were but a mile away
   You would not come.

Jessie B. Rittenhouse

I SHALL BREAK A HEAVY BOUGH

I SHALL break a heavy bough
   With the rain of April wet,
   To carry home and so forget
That there is no beauty now.

Down the ways that I have known,
   Drenched in a reality,
   Every tree will be a tree,
Every stone will be a stone.

Rain that rains and wind that stings
   Will mean nothing more to me
   Than rain and wind — insensibly
All things will be only things.

I shall break an April bough
  To forgetting — it will be
  Easier this way for me —
Hearing, seeing, nothing now!

                    Gertrude Callaghan

THE TIME WHEN I WAS PLOWING

THE time when I was plowing
The fields and days were long,
The weeds went back forever
And the morning-glory clung;
Behind the rumps of horses
The sod ran off forever,
With earth the share was bright;
The sod ran off forever,
The days ran into night.

The time when I was seeding
With rain in the wind
The fields and farms were endless
Under the sky's end.
Here with the disks' turning
And with the horses' treading
A white noon was unending
And time was out of mind.

The times when I was binding
The fields and hours were wide;
Clear to the utter sunset
My sheaves lay side by side;
And life was long as seeming
In a dusk falling,
And in the road the dust was brown
With wagons going up to town.

The time I drove my wagon
Beside a tradesman's door
I dropped the reins and left it
Nor reaped or seeded more;
And years are copper pennies
Dwindling to a score.

Maxwell Anderson

BENEDICTION

LET no blasphemer till the sacred earth
Or scatter seed upon it,
Lest fruit should fail
And weed-scars sting its fineness.

Send him here who loves its beauty
And its brownness.

He will plow the earth
As a dancer dances —
Ecstatically.

Let no blasphemer till the sacred earth
Or scatter seed upon it.

Mark Turbyfill

MIRACLES

IT is a miracle to me
Whence the crooked apple tree
Draws his rough and russet fruit.
Fungus mould is at his root,
And beneath lie only speckled
Granite ridges that thrust freckled
Boulders up for stony fare.
And through the long Winter where

Are willow-kits and daffodils
And marsh-frogs which the Spring earth spills?
Roses, cabbages, and corn,
Pansies and cradled beans are born
All from rain and crumbled rock.
When the tulip with soft shock
Breaks the April-pliant earth,
'Tis as wonderful a birth
Out of black and misty mould
As when hearth-logs bloom in gold!

E. Merrill Root

FOUR LITTLE FOXES

Speak gently, Spring, and make no sudden sound;
For in my windy valley, yesterday I found
New-born foxes squirming on the ground —
       Speak gently.

Walk softly, March, forbear the bitter blow;
Her feet within a trap, her blood upon the snow,
The four little foxes saw their mother go —
       Walk softly.

Go lightly, Spring, oh, give them no alarm;
When I covered them with boughs to shelter them
     from harm,
The thin blue foxes suckled at my arm —
       Go lightly.

Step softly, March, with your rampant hurricane;
Nuzzling one another, and whimpering with pain,
The new little foxes are shivering in the rain —
       Step softly.

Lew Sarett

CAROLINA SPRING SONG

AGAINST the swart magnolias' sheen
Pronged maples, like a stag's new horn,
Stand gouted red upon the green,
In March when shaggy buds are shorn.

Then all a mist-streaked, sunny day
The long sea-islands lean to hear
A water harp that shallows play
To lull the beaches' fluted ear.

When this same music wakes the gift
Of pregnant beauty in the sod,
And makes uneasy vultures shift
Like evil things afraid of God,

Then, then it is I love to drift
Upon the flood-tide's lazy swirls,
While from the level rice fields lift
The spiritu'ls of darky girls.

I hear them singing in the fields
Like voices from the long-ago;
They speak to me of somber worlds
And sorrows that the humble know;

Of sorrow — yet their tones release
A harmony of larger hours
From easy epochs long at peace
Amid an irony of flowers.

So if they sometimes seem a choir
That cast a chill of doubt on spring,
They have still higher notes of fire
Like cardinals upon the wing.

Hervey Allen

36848

SPRING MORNING — SANTA FÉ

THE first hour was a word the color of dawn ;
The second came, and gorgeous poppies stood
Backs to the wall.   The yellow sun rode on :
A mockingbird sang from a nest of wood.

The water in the acequia came down
At the stroke of nine, and watery clouds were lifting
Their velvet shadows from the little town :
Gold fired the pavement where the leaves were shift-
      ing.

At ten, black shawls of women bowed along
The Alameda.   Sleepy burros lay
In the heat, and lifted up their ears.   A song
Wavered upon the wind and died away,

And the great bells rang out a golden tune :
Words grew in the heart and clanged, the color of
      noon.

Lynn Riggs

APRIL'S AMAZING MEANING

APRIL'S amazing meaning doubtless lies
   In tall, hoarse boys and slips
Of slender girls with suddenly wider eyes
   And parted lips ;

For girls must wander pensive in the spring
   When the green rain is over,
Doing some slow inconsequential thing,
   Plucking clover ;

And any boy alone upon a bench
  When his work's done will sit
And stare at the black ground and break a branch
  And whittle it

Slowly; and boys and girls, irresolute,
  Will curse the dreamy weather
Until they meet past the pale hedge and put
  Their lips together.

George H. Dillon

LOST — AN APRIL

How can new Aprils come, when one was lost
  Out of the withering gold of all the years —
Brief fires burned to silver of long frost;
  Spent ardors cooled in quietude of tears?

Last year I knew the beauty of a sea
  Where faded cities hold an opal dream,
And climbed warm olive slopes of Italy,
  And walked in Egypt by a glamorous stream.

These lands know starlight beautiful as death,
  And year long wear their ardent colors still, —
Oh, shall there come again the March wind's breath,
  And wild arbutus on a waiting hill?

How can they truly know the rapturous Spring,
  If Beauty never lies upon a bier?
Oh, magic past the heart's imagining,
  In that one April that I lost last year!

Mary Brent Whiteside

HEAVEN YOU SAY WILL BE A FIELD IN APRIL

HEAVEN, you say, will be a field in April,
A friendly field, a long green wave of earth,
With one domed cloud above it. There you'll lie
In noon's delight, with bees to flash above you,
Drown amid buttercups that blaze in the wind,
Forgetting all save beauty. There you'll see
With sun-filled eyes your one great dome of cloud
Adding fantastic towers and spires of light,
Ascending, like a ghost, to melt in the blue.
Heaven enough, in truth, if you were there!
Could I be with you, I would choose your noon,
Drown amid buttercups, laugh with the intimate
    grass,
Dream there forever. . . . But, being older, sadder,
Having not you, nor aught save thought of you,
It is not spring I'll choose, but fading summer;
Not noon I'll choose, but the charmed hour of dusk.
Poppies? A few! And a moon almost as red.
But most I'll choose that subtler dusk that comes
Into the mind — into the heart, you say —
When as we look bewildered at lovely things,
Striving to give their loveliness a name,
They are forgotten; and other things, remembered,
Flower in the heart with the fragrance we call grief.
Conrad Aiken

BEYOND

I WONDER if the tides of Spring
    Will always bring me back again
Mute rapture at the simple thing
    Of lilacs blowing in the rain.

If so, my heart will ever be
Above all fear, for I shall know
There is a greater mystery
Beyond the time when lilacs blow.

Thomas S. Jones, Jr.

LILACS

AFTER lilacs come out
The air loves to flow about them
The way water in wood-streams
Flows and loves and wanders.
I think the wind has a sadness
Lifting other leaves, other sprays . . .
I think the wind is a little selfish
About lilacs when they flower.

Hilda Conkling

LILACS

LILACS,
False blue,
White,
Purple,
Colour of lilac,
Your great puffs of flowers
Are everywhere in this my New England.
Among your heart-shaped leaves
Orange orioles hop like music-box birds and sing
Their little weak soft songs;
In the crooks of your branches
The bright eyes of song sparrows sitting on spotted
  eggs
Peer restlessly through the light and shadow
Of all Springs.
Lilacs in dooryards

Holding quiet conversations with an early moon;
Lilacs watching a deserted house
Settling sideways into the grass of an old road;
Lilacs, wind-beaten, staggering under a lopsided shock
    of bloom
Above a cellar dug into a hill.
You are everywhere.
You were everywhere.
You tapped the window when the preacher preached
    his sermon,
And ran along the road beside the boy going to school.
You stood by pasture-bars to give the cows good milk-
    ing,
You persuaded the housewife that her dish pan was of
    silver
And her husband an image of pure gold.
You flaunted the fragrance of your blossoms
Through the wide doors of Custom Houses —
You, and sandal-wood, and tea,
Charging the noses of quill-driving clerks
When a ship was in from China.
You called to them: "Goose-quill men, goose-quill
    men,
May is a month for flitting,"
Until they writhed on their high stools
And wrote poetry on their letter-sheets behind the
    propped-up ledgers.
Paradoxical New England clerks,
Writing inventories in ledgers, reading the "Song of
    Solomon" at night,
So many verses before bed-time,
Because it was the Bible.
The dead fed you
Amid the slant stones of graveyards.

Pale ghosts who planted you
Came in the night-time
And let their thin hair blow through your clustered
    stems.
You are of the green sea,
And of the stone hills which reach a long distance.
You are of elm-shaded streets with little shops where
    they sell kites and marbles,
You are of great parks where everyone walks and
    nobody is at home.
You cover the blind sides of greenhouses
And lean over the top to say a hurry-word through
    the glass
To your friends, the grapes, inside.

Lilacs,
False blue,
White,
Purple,
Colour of lilac,
You have forgotten your Eastern origin,
The veiled women with eyes like panthers,
The swollen, aggressive turbans of jewelled **Pashas.**
Now you are a very decent flower,
A reticent flower,
A curiously clear-cut, candid flower,
Standing beside clean doorways,
Friendly to a house-cat and a pair of spectacles,
Making poetry out of a bit of moonlight
And a hundred or two sharp blossoms.

Maine knows you,
Has for years and years;
New Hampshire knows you,

And Massachusetts
And Vermont.
Cape Cod starts you along the beaches to Rhode
     Island;
Connecticut takes you from a river to the sea.
You are brighter than apples,
Sweeter than tulips,
You are the great flood of our souls
Bursting above the leaf-shapes of our hearts,
You are the smell of all Summers,
The love of wives and children,
The recollection of the gardens of little children,
You are State Houses and Charters
And the familiar treading of the foot to and fro on a
     road it knows.
May is lilac here in New England,
May is a thrush singing "Sun up!" on a tip-top ash-
     tree,
May is white clouds behind pine-trees
Puffed out and marching upon a blue sky.
May is a green as no other,
May is much sun through small leaves,
May is soft earth,
And apple-blossoms,
And windows open to a South wind.
May is a full light wind of lilac
From Canada to Narragansett Bay.

Lilacs,
False blue,
White,
Purple,
Colour of lilac.
Heart-leaves of lilac all over New England,

Roots of lilac under all the soil of New England,
Lilac in me because I am New England,
Because my roots are in it,
Because my leaves are of it,
Because my flowers are for it,
Because it is my country
And I speak to it of itself
And sing of it with my own voice
Since certainly it is mine.

Amy Lowell

SPRING IN TOWN

Spring comes to town like some mad girl, who runs
With silver feet upon the Avenue,
And, like Ophelia, in her tresses twines
The first young blossoms — purple violets
And golden daffodils.   These are enough —
These fragile handfuls of miraculous bloom —
To make the monster City feel the Spring!
One dash of color on her dun-gray hood,
One flash of yellow near her pallid face,
And she and April are the best of friends —
Benighted town that needs a friend so much!
How she responds to that first soft caress,
And draws the hoyden Spring close to her heart,
And thrills and sings, and for one little time
Forgets the foolish panic of her sons,
Forgets her sordid merchandise and trade,
And lightly trips while hurdy-gurdies ring —
A wise old crone upon a holiday!

Charles Hanson Towne

OLD MEADOWS

How much we have forgotten that we knew!
The warmth of udders, and the cool of dew,
The flow of darkness when the sun goes down —
We have forgotten meadows in the town —
The sign of beasts, the easy lilt of wings;
We miss the miracle of usual things.

Once we were one with daily mysteries,
Trusting the arms in which our life began;
Earth in the cloudy nursery of high hills
Unswathed her mountain breasts to infant man,
But now her meadows' calm beatitudes
Are stifled by the city's platitudes,
And we forget Earth's hills, her ocean faces,
And the austere-grotesquery of desert places.

Yet, it is true, beneath the city's robe
The desecrated pastures dream of stars
That still behold from quiet places
The ocean-staring, sun-bathed globe
Slip through the nether spaces.
In the night interludes, when streets are solitudes,
They sleep and wait, dreaming of Ilium's fate,
And of the grass that time will reinstate.

Old fields bear epochs patiently, but men
Cannot abide till towns grow trees again,
And so they ravish Beauty for their joy,
And bring her home as Helen came to Troy,
A prisoner to the chisel or the pen.
But in the town she walks a stolen bride,
And only plays at marriage with the throng;

She lives in thrall, and gazes homesick from the city
    wall,
While Earth's wild genius fights against the wrong.

Long cataracts of streets make us forget
That underneath the stones are ancient fields
Which whisper to the feet of Beauty yet
A longing for the grass until she yields.
And even while we claim her gratitude
For building her a house in which to die,
She seeks green solitude,
Where shepherds pipe in an eternal mood,
And daffs the mad world by.

Hervey Allen

SONNETS FROM A HOSPITAL

SPRING

REMEMBERING sunlight on the steepled square,
    Remembering April's way with little streets,
And pouter pigeons coasting down the air,
    Spilling a beauty like white-crested fleets, —
I have imagined, in these pain-racked days,
    The look of grasses thrusting through the earth,
Of tender shoots along green-bordered ways,
    Of hedges, and their first, frail blossoming mirth.

I have imagined, too, in some such wise
    Death may allow, within her darkened room,
Some subtle intimation of wide skies,
    Of startled grasses, and the hedge in bloom, —
And we may know when some far spring comes down,
Wearing her magic slippers through the town.

David Morton

ALONE IN SPRING

I NEVER met the Spring alone before,
The flowers, birds, the loveliness of trees,
For with me always there was one I love
And love is shield against such gifts as these.
But now I am alone, alone, alone,
The days and nights one long remembering.
Did other Aprils that we shared possess
The hurting beauty of this living Spring?
I never met the Spring alone before:
My starving grief, this radiance of gold!
To be alone, when Spring is being born,
One should be dead —

> or suddenly grown old.
> *Caroline Giltinan*

COME FORTH! FOR SPRING IS SINGING IN THE BOUGHS

COME forth! for Spring is singing in the boughs
Of every white and tremulous apple-tree.
This is the season of eternal vows;
Yet what are vows that they should solace me?
For on the winds, wild loveliness is crying;
And in all flowers, wild joy its present worth
Proclaims, as from the dying to the dying —
"Seize, clasp your hour of sun upon the earth!"
Then never dream that fire or beauty stays
More than one April moment in its flight
Toward regions where the sea-drift of all days
Sinks in a vast, desireless, lonely night.
O wind from flushing orchards! — give me breath
Of one white hour here on the marge of death!

> *Arthur Davison Ficke*

SONG OF THE LONG RIVER

ALL day my songs
Sang beside the River,
Sang on my lips like my lover's kiss.
I asked no more:
  "Tell me, how long, Sky, how long is the **River**
That flows on and on yet stays forever,
Bearing my songs oh whither, whither?"

I said only: —
  "When the starry wampum is offered,
When the twilight smoke signals
That the woman, Swiya, camps beneath the willows
And her tent of willows,
Is open — is open — open. . . .
Will he come, the Man of Arrows,
Like a white hawk skimming
Down the circling path of waters,
Down the tide
Of the silver singing River,
That winds — and, winding, beckons —
Like a low-hung girdle round the hills?"

I said only:
  "Come! Swift and Wounding One, to my lips.
When the two crimson wings,
The wings of my flying Song, are folded!

The flesh of my songs is sweeter, O Wounding One,
Than wild turkeys;
Softer than feathers is Swiya's breast, swelling with
      love.

Moor thy white canoe
By the running River

Till lily-picker Dawn shall pluck it
From the black-tipped clustering bulrushes of night.
Leave the shallower tide
Of the silver singing River, for the deeper flowing;
Leap to the still-winged silence of thy mate!"

When the starry wampum is offered,
When the twilight smoke signals
That the woman, Swiya, camps beneath the willows;
And her tent of willows,
Red spring willows,
Is open — is open — open —. . . .

Constance Lindsay Skinner

DISCOVERY

UNTIL my lamp and I
Stood close together by the glass,
I had not ever noticed
I was a comely lass.

My aunts have always nodded,
"Sweet child,
She has a gentle soul
And mild."

And so, one night,
I took the lamp and said,
"I'll look upon my gentle soul
Before I go to bed."

I could not find it — no —
But gazing hard I spied
Something much more near to me,
White-armed and amber-eyed.

And as I looked I seemed to feel
Warm hands upon my breast,
Where never any hands but mine
Were known to rest.

And as I looked, my startled thoughts
Winged up in happy flight,
And circled like mad butterflies
About the light.

I went to bed without my soul
And I had no mind to care,
For a joyful little sin
Slept pillowed on my hair.

I went to bed without my soul —
What difference to me?
I had a joyful little sin
For company.

And that is what came of listening
To aunts who always lied.
They never told me that I was
White-armed and amber-eyed.

Hildegarde Flanner

BLUE GIRLS

TWIRLING your blue skirts, travelling the sward
Under the towers of your seminary,
Go listen to your teachers old and contrary
Without believing a word.

Tie the white fillets then about your lustrous hair
And think no more of what will come to pass
Than bluebirds that go walking on the grass
And chattering on the air.

Practise your beauty, blue girls, before it fail;
And I will cry with my loud lips and publish
Beauty which all our power shall never establish,
It is so frail.

For I could tell you a story which is true:
I know a lady with a terrible tongue,
Blear eyes fallen from blue,
All her perfections tarnished — and yet it is not long
Since she was lovelier than any of you.

John Crowe Ransom

WOMAN

I HAVE known a woman
Before she ever spoke,
By the colors of her scarf;
The way she wore her cloak.

You that talk against earth
How do you dare
Slander one who scatters
Stars in her hair?

Is she not good who chooses
Fillet of the leaves,
Who wears meadow-velvet
For her green sleeves?

Isabel Fiske Conant

DON JUAN IN PORTUGAL

AT every pelourinho's ledge
Faces to set my teeth on edge;
Gray gossips like a cactus hedge
Whisper and crackle.

I lean at Alcobaca, dim
Carved fig-leaves twisted round its rim
And Indian snakes.   Pauses a slim
Tall maid. . . .   Her name?   A Latin hymn, —

Gloria de Madre de Deus,
A white-rose face dipped tremulous,
Profile carved as nobly clear
As love-child of Aurelius.

White-clad, bare-legged, straight she stood,
Vase-bearing nymph ripe to be wooed
In some delicious interlude.

What need now to remember more?
The tiled and twisted fountain's pour,
The vase forgotten on the floor,
The white street ending in her door.

Her head, a dark flower on its stem;
Her diadem
Of heavy hair, the Moorish low estalegem.

Outside, the stillness and white glare
Of Alcobaca's noonday square.
My hands that dare.
The beauty of her loosened hair.

White shift, white door, the white still street, —
Her lips, her arms, her throat, her feet, —
— After a while, some bread and meat.

A dewy jar of cool red wine,
Olives that glisten wet with brine.
White rose of Alcobaca, mine!
We kiss again above the wine.

The red wine drunk, the broken crust,
We parted as all lovers must.
Madre in Gloria, be Thou just
To that frail glory,
A white rose fallen into dust.

Florence Wilkinson

THE LAST NIGHT

HADN'T we better rise and go
    Down to the wood so ashen-white?
And you will give me a kiss I know
    Since this is our last night.

I will give you a kiss indeed,
    A kiss for this and a kiss for that!
And maybe a kiss to fill your need —
    So go and get your hat.

This place is best of all, I think,
    With the white star-blossoms in the grass,
And a whip-poor-will may come to drink,
    But never a body pass.

This place is well enough, indeed,
    To bind my soul and senses quite,
For I shall never again be freed
    From the kiss I give to-night.

Orrick Johns

WHAT LIPS MY LIPS HAVE KISSED

WHAT lips my lips have kissed, and where, and why,
I have forgotten, and what arms have lain
Under my head till morning; but the rain
Is full of ghosts to-night, that tap and sigh
Upon the glass and listen for reply,

And in my heart there stirs a quiet pain
For unremembered lads that not again
Will turn to me at midnight with a cry.
Thus in the winter stands the lonely tree,
Nor knows what birds have vanished one by one,
Yet knows its boughs more silent than before:
I cannot say what loves have come and gone,
I only know that summer sang in me
A little while, that in me sings no more.

Edna St. Vincent Millay

ILLIMITABLE

PARTING love, far-fled content,
　　Illimitable woe —
For a thousand kisses spent,
　　Kiss me, and I will go.

Age with all its wrinkled fret
　　Waits us ere we know,
Age, the nurse of pale regret —
　　Kiss me, and I will go.

Gamaliel Bradford

GIVE ME NO LOVER YOUNG WITH LOVE

GIVE me no lover young with love.
I would not be
Enthroned in any heart as queen
Of such doomed ecstasy.

Give me a lover old with grief,
Lonely and wise.
Perhaps I could lift sadness
From his eyes.

Lucia Trent

BY AN IRIS-SHADOWED POOL

YOUR hot mouth on mine is good;
But so is the cool wood.

So are the cool stars — and the cool
Iris-shadowed pool.

I can live with them alone,
Cool grass and cool stone;
But if your mouth take from me these,
I had rather cool trees,
Cool stars, and cool
Grass in a rainy breeze.
Yes, even the little pool.

Mary Carolyn Davies

TO A BROWN GIRL

WHAT if his glance is bold and free,
  His mouth the lash of whips?
So should the eyes of lovers be,
  And so a lover's lips.

What if no puritanic strain
  Confines him to the nice?
He will not pass this way again,
  Nor hunger for you twice.

Since in the end consort together
  Magdalen and Mary,
Youth is the time for careless weather:
  Later, lass, be wary.

Countee Cullen

BALLAD OF THE DOORSTONE

I wet my feet in the river
And it's here I must stay
Close to my doorstone
Forever and a day,
So they say. . . .

All day and all day
I watched my da's sheep,
Helped them with their lambing,
Huddled them to sleep.

And all day and all day
I watched the three cows,
Coaxed their lazy udders,
Turned them out to browse.

But my thoughts were wild ducks
And off they would fly
Over the bog
To the scruff of the sky,

And my wild duck thoughts
Beat their windy wings,
Though my body bided here
Minding other things.

There fell a day in April.
My ducks swarmed the sky,
Destroyed I was with milking cows
And wished I could die,
Or their dugs go dry.

And then . . . came the beat
Of hoofs upon the turf,

Skeltering hoofs that mounted
Like pounding surf,

And out through the furze
A horse plunged by
Flinging in the ditch
Something to die,
Something strange to die.

God help me, he was proud to see!
A rider of the world,
The whisht of death upon his face,
His hair bright-curled,
The jewel of the world.

He was flung there to die,
But my arms made his bed,
My breath breathed him back
From the shiftless dead.

You'll die, and I'll die,
But he'll die — never.
He'll laugh and ride and kiss
Foralways and forever.

Too soon it was I cured him.
He stood up like a tree,
His curling hair was bright as brass,
His breast the height of me.

All day and all day
He helped me tend the sheep,
Taught me April's ways,
Her tryst to keep.

And all night and all night
We counted the stars.

Oh, I wouldn't trade my lot
For all its scars
And its pasture bars.

I grudged an hour's sleeping.
His saddle would speak,
And time would come he'd gallop off,
God's breath upon his cheek. . . .

And he went so —
In a splendor of hoofs
That sped like arrows
Through the skyey roofs.

A moon of April
Drew him from sight,
Left me shut of laughter
In a blur of night. . . .

All day and all day
I watch my da's sheep;
But things are not the same now:
I've something to keep.

And all night and all night
I think of my dear.
The thought of him is bright as rain
And warm as a tear.

When Winter strides the hillsides
In boots of snow
And shouts down the worldway
His rough hallo,

I'll not be smited with his fist,
Nor think him over-strong.

I'll be taking stitches
A fairy-foot long,
And humming a song.

Oh, I shall be a-borning
My own white lamb.
I'll never let him miss his sire
So close will be his dam.

And when my lad is come a **man**
I'll tell him of his sire,
I'll bid him leave the barley field,
The cows in the byre,

And go where my wild ducks
Fly past the hill,
Leading the way
As wild ducks will.

And he shall know his sire
By his own glad grace.
I'll have no son, I'm telling you,
Without his father's face.

And he'll say, "Your're my da,
And it's I am your lad.
My mother sent me back to you:
I'm everything she had."

Oh, I wet my feet in the river
And it's here I must stay
Close to my doorstone
Foralways and a day,
So they say . . .
So they say . . .

                          Louise Ayres Garnett

TO LOVERS

LAD, will you draw the lightning down
And pluck the morning star from the sky
To light a fire on your hearthstone
That a wilful girl may sit thereby?

Maid, will you harness the eagle's wings
And bit the jaws of the restless foam
And change the cry of the gypsy wind
For the click of a latch when your man comes home?

Swift and sure go the lonely feet,
And the single eye sees cold and true,
And the road that has room and to spare for one
May be sorely narrow for two —

Yet still they light their fire at the stars,
And still they bridle the chafing sea
For the sake of a dream that has always been . . .
That will always be.

Amelia Josephine Burr

SONG FOR UNBOUND HAIR

OH, never marry Ishmael!
Marry another and prosper well;
But not, but never Ishmael. . . .

What has he ever to buy or sell?
He only owns what his strength can keep,
Only a vanishing knot of sheep,
A goat or two.   Does he sow or reap?
In the hanging rocks rings his old ram's bell —
Who would marry Ishmael!

What has he to give to a bride?
Only trouble, little beside,
Only his arm like a little cave
To cover a woman and keep her safe;
A rough fierce kiss, and the wind and rain,
A child, perhaps, and another again —
Who would marry Ishmael?

The arrogant Lucifer when he fell
Bequeathed his wrath to Ishmael;
The hand of every man is set
Against this lad, and this lad's hand
Is cruel and quick, — forget, forget
The nomad boy on his leagues of sand. . . .

Marry another and prosper well,
But not, but never Ishmael.

Genevieve Taggard

PIRATE TREASURE

A LADY loved a swaggering rover;
The seven salt seas he voyaged over,
Bragged of a hoard none could discover,
              Hey! Jolly Roger, O.

She bloomed in a mansion dull and stately,
And as to Meeting she walked sedately,
From the tail of her eye she liked him greatly,
              Hey! Jolly Roger, O.

Rings in his ears and a red sash wore he,
He sang her a song and he told her a story;
"I'll make ye Queen of the Ocean," swore he,
              Hey! Jolly Roger, O.

She crept from bed by her sleeping sister;
By the old gray mill he met and kissed her.
Blue day dawned before they missed her,
    Hey! Jolly Roger, O.

And while they prayed her out of Meeting,
Her wild little heart with bliss was beating,
As seaward went the lugger fleeting,
    Hey! Jolly Roger, O.

Choose in haste and repent at leisure;
A buccaneer life is not all pleasure.
He set her ashore with a little treasure,
    Hey! Jolly Roger, O.

Off he sailed where waves were dashing,
Knives were gleaming, cutlasses clashing,
And a ship on jagged rocks went crashing,
    Hey! Jolly Roger, O.

Over his bones the tides are sweeping;
The only trace of the rover sleeping
Is what he left in the lady's keeping,
    Hey! Jolly Roger, O.

Two hundred years is his name unspoken,
The secret of his hoard unbroken;
But a black-browed race wears the pirate's token,
    Hey! Jolly Roger, O.
              Abbie Farwell Brown

A BARGE WIFE

How many days now is it we have lain
Here by the towering docks? — I do not know;
Each day, eager and free, the sail-boats go

Out to the west. I would go swiftly, too,
Like a bird at dawn across the opening blue,
Like a bird — to rest again.

He has grown silent with the years — men do —
Having talked the same thing much. For my part
     now
It is enough to watch the huge boats plow
Furrows of white ; to cook, to sew, to hear
Her little laughing voice ! Yet God, I fear
Lest she be barge-wed, too.

                              John Farrar

A HILL-WOMAN

You'd think I'd hate the hills ? — well, this life brings
Little that's new.   Once many years ago
I thought I'd leave the place and flee below,
Down where the world is bright with life and change,
But I met him, and now — it's very strange
How marriage changes things.

Listen ! — beyond that grove (you would not know)
A hermit thrush, it sings round five each night !
One moment now, and *he* will come in sight
Driving the chestnut mare ! There, that's his call !
I hate the hills ?   How could I, now, at all,
Knowing he loves me so ?

                              John Farrar

THE DOOR

Love is a proud and gentle thing, a better thing to own
Than all of the wide impossible stars over the heavens
     blown,

And the little gifts her hand gives are careless given
    or taken,
And though the whole great world break, the heart
    of her is not shaken. . . .
Love is a viol in the wind, a viol never stilled,
And mine of all is the surest that ever time has willed.
I shall speak to her though she goes before me into the
    grave,
And though I drown in the sea, herself shall laugh
    upon a wave;
And the things that love gives after shall be as they
    were before,
For life is only a small house . . . and love is an open
    door.

Orrick Johns

MATERNITY

I MUST go all my days
Softly as snow, whose wings
Follow the hidden ways
Of unimagined springs.

My stricken heart is caught
In briers of surprise;
Its beats are hushed as thought,
And eloquent as eyes.

I cry God pity them
Whose joy is boisterous,
Since I have touched the hem
Of the miraculous.

Babette Deutch

TRIBUTE

DEBORAH and Christopher brought me dandelions,
　Kenton brought me buttercups with summer on
　　　their breath,
But Michael brought an autumn leaf, like lacy filigree,
　A wan leaf, a ghost leaf, beautiful as death.

Death in all loveliness, fragile and exquisite,
　Who but he would choose it from all the blossoming
　　　land?
Who but he would find it where it hid among the
　　　flowers?
　Death in all loveliness, he laid it in my hand.
　　　　　　　　　　　　　Aline Kilmer

MATER IN EXTREMIS

I STAND between them and the outer winds,
But I am a crumbling wall.
They told me they could bear the blast alone,
They told me: that was all.
But I must wedge myself between
Them and the first snowfall.

Riddled am I by onslaughts and attacks
I thought I could forestall,
I reared and braced myself to shelter them
Before I heard them call.
I cry them, God, a better shield!
I am about to fall.
　　　　　　　　　　　Jean Starr Untermeyer

THE HOUSE AT EVENING

Across the school-ground it would start
To light my eyes, that yellow gleam, —
The window of the flaming heart,
The chimney of the tossing dream,
The scuffed and wooden porch of Heaven,
The voice that came like a caress,
The warm kind hands that once were given
My carelessness.

It was a house you would not think
Could hold such sacraments in things
Or give the wild heart meat and drink
Or give the stormy soul high wings
Or chime small voices to such mirth
Or crown the night with stars and flowers
Or make upon this quaking earth
Such steady hours.

Yet, that in storm it stood secure,
And in the cold was warm with love,
Shall its similitude endure
Past trophies that men weary of,
When two were out of fortune's reach,
Building great empires round a name
And ushering into casual speech
Dim worlds aflame.

William Rose Benét

EXILE

She would have liked the smallest things,
Thin tea-cups, thimbles, garden-swings,
Ribbons and laces, tiny shoes in rows :

She must put up though, with the grandiose —
With prairies, forests, mountain ranges, snows;
These walk with her, these with a friendly charm
Can tuck themselves beneath her arm;
But there is a remembrance like a scar
Of having dreamed once of the little things
Forgetting vast things are.

Kathryn White Ryan

MY MOTHER'S HOUSE

"It's strange," my mother said, "to think
Of the old house where we were born.
I can remember every chink
And every board our feet had worn.

"It's gone now.   Many years ago
They tore it down.   It was too old,
And none too grand as houses go,
Not like a new house, bought or sold.

"And so they tore it down.   But we
Could talk about it still, and say
'Just so the kitchen used to be,
And the stairs turned in such a way.'

"But we're gone too now.   Everyone
Who knew the house is dead and buried.
And I'll not last so long alone
With all my children grown and married.

"There's not a living soul can tell,
Except myself, just how the grass
Grew round the pathway to the well,
Or where the china-closet was.

"Yet while I live you cannot say
That the old house is quite, quite dead.
It still exists in some dim way
While I remember it," she said.

Eunice Tietjens

TRAVEL'S END

O BED in my mother's house,
    With sheets as white as May,
With blankets wove of the carded wool
    And scented with new-mown hay.

With the poke of feather down
    From her snow-white plumy geese;
O bed of mine in my mother's house,
    With sleep that was dreamy peace.

Far have I walked forlorn,
    O bed that my mother made;
I would that your sheet might be my shroud
    And I in earth be laid.

May Folwell Hoisington

INHERITANCE

THEY left to me their house and lands
Who am the next of kin,
On what was theirs I lay my hands
And freely I go in.

Before the hearth where they once sat
I speak my yes and no,
I am the master over it
That once would come and go.

I would repeat the bitter sting
Of all my early need,
Yes, I would own not anything
But have them here indeed.

I would resign my years of right
If I could hear them say :
"We cannot let you go tonight,"
Or, "Come and spend the day."

Now my estate lies broad and fair
As far as eye can see,
But not a voice breaks on the air
And no one speaks to me.

Anna Hempstead Branch

BALLAD OF A LOST HOUSE

I

Hungry Heart, Hungry Heart, where have you been?
I've been to a town where lives a queen.

Hungry Heart, Hungry Heart, what did you there?
I ran all the way to a certain Square.

Hungry Heart, say what you did that for!
To find a street and a certain door;
And there I knocked my knuckles sore.

II

That was a foolish thing to do,
Alone in the night the long hours through;

Gaping there like a chalky clown
At a stranger-door that had been your own.

Where was your pluck and where your pride?
They both were there, and love beside;
And suddenly the door swung wide.

I heard the sound of a violin
That seemed to bid me enter in:

For a fiddle's a key for many a lock,
And will open a door though it's built in rock.

III

Tell me, Hungry, what did you see?
A lighted hall where friends made free.

I trod with them a well-known stair —
How did you dare, Heart! How did you dare?

For a frowning face you may trust and like,
But who shall say when a smile will strike?

IV

Up the oaken stair went I,
And all made way to let me by.

Some reached a hand and some looked down,
But I never saw their smile nor frown.

I never saw familiar things
That sought me with quaint beckonings:

The carven saints in postures mild,
Kind Virgins with the Heavenly Child,

Ladies and Knights in tapestries —
I never saw nor looked at these.

Only the Christ from a canvas dim,
Drooping there on His leafless Limb;
He looked at me and I looked at Him.

V

Where did you go, old Unafraid?
Up to a place where children played —
The happy hubbub the small three made!

Patter and prattle and toys and games,
Dolls in rows with curious names,

Voices lifted like high thin tunes,
Lively suppers with round-tipped spoons!

Where should I go but up the stair
To the welcome I knew was waiting there?

But all was dark, as only can be
A long deserted nursery;
And never a sound to succor me.

VI

So I turned to a room where a woman slept
In a gay gold bed, and near I crept,

And lingered and listened — oh anguished morn,
Oh flute cry of a babe new-born,
Clearer than trumpeting Gabriel's horn!

Oh sea of Life, with Love for a chart —
On with the tale, old Hungry Heart!

VII

On with the tale and on to a door
Where a man had passed to pass no more:

A quiet man with a quiet strength,
And over the threshold his shadow's length

Lay like an answer for Time to weigh;
And the dust from his feet spread thick and grey.

And I thought: Well shaken! Let friend or foe
Sweep up the dust an it please them so;

Let Lord and Valet tend to the room;
Lady, and House-maid, here with the broom!

Bid Town and Tattle see to it too
That the windows be washed of the mud they threw.

Dust and ashes of what has been!
Sweep the clean house.   And keep it clean.

VIII

I thought to curse — but strange, a prayer
Rose to my lips as I stood there.

And this my praying: Now all good cheer
To him who sleeps where slept my dear,
For the sake of the good dreams once dreamed here.

IX

Back to the stair and down I sped,
Passing a loud room table-spread;

Passing, but pausing, as house-wives do,
Judging the viands that came to view;

Trusting the sauce was tuned to the meat,
The wine well cooled and the pudding sweet;

Pausing, but passing —

Stay, Heart of mine,
What of the guests?   For I divine
Their looks were grand and their manners fine.

X

A goodly company, I'll admit,
And some had beauty and some had wit —

And some you loved?   Well, what of it?

And some loved you!   Perhaps, perhaps,
With linen napkins in their laps,

With cups that foamed and piled-up plates;
They loved me with a hundred hates!

They hated in such lovely ways,
With laughter, singing, kisses, praise —

How could I know?   How could I know?
Hungry Heart, Hungry Heart, cry not so!

XI

And as I lingered watching them,
I felt a tugging at my hem;

My little dog was cowering there,
A glassy terror in its stare;

My veins turned ice — O smacking lips,
O dainty greedy finger-tips!

'Twas bones of Hungry Heart they ate,
Broken and boiled and delicate,

Platter on platter the board along,
And as they supped they sang a song:

An ancient ardent melody
About a lady passing by
Whom they must love until they die

XII

And as they drank I saw the wine,
It never came from ripened vine,

It never was brewed in tub or vat,
Knew web of spider or squeak of rat —
But it knows their thirst and it pours for that.

A thirsty stream that none may gauge,
That none shall slake though the stream assuage,

Of wine the very counterpart,
Out of the side of Hungry Heart.

And mixed with the toast, a violin,
Mellow and merry above the din,
Held shoulder high 'neath a woman's chin.

XIII

Hungry Heart, come, make haste, make haste,
Out of the house of hopes laid waste,

Out of the town of teeth laid bare
Under its smiling debonair.

Wait not, weep not, get you gone,
Better the stones to rest upon,

The wind and the rain for a roof secure,
Hyssop and tares for your nouriture:
These shall endure.   These shall endure.

XIV

I got me gone.   On stumbling feet
I reached the stair and I reached the street;

The door slammed to with an iron scream,
And behind it lay the end of a dream;

Behind it lifted barren walls,
And I thought of a play when the curtain falls
On a comedy written of shrouds and palls.

XV

Hungry Heart, Hungry Heart, what did you then?
I fell on my knees and I cried, Amen!
But now and again — now and again —

I come to the door in the dead of night,
I wander the rooms till the panes are white;

A landlord ghost! Aye, one who knows
His lease outlived with the cock that crows,
A wraith content that contented goes.

Goes at the cry of the bird unseen,
Calling the friends of what has been;

And some it names lie sleeping near —
Ah, wake them not, friend Chanticleer!

XVI

Three times it calls the end of the dream,
And still I return, for still I seem

To comfort a house that lives aloof
From all who live beneath its roof.

I must return! to dispossess
Those bartered walls of loneliness:

Mortar and brick and iron and bole,
Where all may pass who pay their toll;
The husk of a house that has lost its soul.

XVII

For out of that house went its soul with me,
Leaping and crying after me,
To bear me faithful company
Over a clear and quickening sea.

                              Leonora Speyer

OUT OF BABYLON

As I stole out of Babylon beyond the stolid warders,
    (My soul that dwelt in Babylon long, long ago)
The sound of cymbals and of lutes, of viols and re-
        corders,
    Came up from khan and caravan, loud and low.

As I crept out of Babylon the clangor and the babel,
    The strife of life, the haggling in the square and
        mart,

Of the men who went in saffron and the men who
    went in sable,
  It tore me and it wore me, yea, it wore my heart.

As I fled out of Babylon the cubits of the towers
  They seemed in very mockery to bar my way;
The incense of the altars and the hanging-garden
    flowers,
  They lured me with their glamour, but I would not
    stay.

We still flee out of Babylon, its vending and its vying,
  Its crying up to Mammon, its bowing to Baal;
We still flee out of Babylon, its sobbing and its sigh-
    ing,
  Where the strong grow ever stronger, and the weary
    fail.

We still flee out of Babylon, the feverish, the fretful,
  That saps the sweetness of the soul and leaves but
    a rind;
We still flee out of Babylon, and fain would be for-
    getful
  Of all within that girdling wall threatening behind.

Oh, Babylon, oh, Babylon, your toiling and your
    teeming,
  Your canyons and your wonder-wealth, — not for
    such as we!
We who have fled from Babylon contented are with
    dreaming,
  Dreaming of earth's loveliness, happy to be free!
                    Clinton Scollard

THE ABBOT OF DERRY

THE Abbot of Derry
  Hates Satan and Sin;
'Tis strange of him, very;
  They're both his blood-kin;
And the Devil go bury the Abbot of Derry,
  And bury him deep, say I!

The Abbot of Derry
  Has woman nor wine.
'Tis kind of him, very,
  To leave them all mine:
And the Devil go bury the Abbot of Derry,
  And bury him deep, say I!

Says the Abbot of Derry:
  "To-morrow ye die!"
"Eat, drink, and be merry!"
  Say Dolly and I:
And the Devil go bury the Abbot of Derry,
  And bury him deep, say I!

The Abbot of Derry
  Says "All flesh is grass."
Sure, the Abbot should know,
  For the Abbot's an ass!
And the Devil go bury the Abbot of Derry,
  And bury him deep, say I!

The Abbot of Derry
  Says "Love is a knave!"
I shall love when the Abbot
  Lies deep in his grave: —
And the Devil go bury the Abbot of Derry,
  And bury him deep, say I!

John Bennett

FROM ALL THE FOOLS WHO WENT BEFORE'

FROM all the fools who went before
  I learned a wealth of wit!
For over Wisdom's darkest door
  Some fool a lamp had lit.

Ye shun, O Sages overwise,
  Experience's school,
And lose the lore — for which he dies —
  Gained by some gallant fool!

Margaret Root Garvin

THE PLAYBOX

THE toys of a Tutankhamen
  Are under the king's high chair;
The Queen hath her doll-house in order
  With all of the miniatures there.

But sometimes they sigh for the splendors —
  The strays of the playbox hoard,
The light of a Nightingale lantern,
  The glimmer of Arthur's sword.

The bugle of Balaklava,
  The pipes in the Havelock van,
The faith of a gearless Godiva,
  The ending to Kubla Khan.

Though lost in the dominant seventh
  The hunters are down on their knees;
They are after the strays of the playbox,
  For Luxor had nothing like these.

Nathalia Crane

TO MY TERRIER REX

Each night before I sleep,
  Out of doors I steal,
Upon the shore to watch
  The Constellations wheel —
  My terrier at heel —

To learn the lore of night,
  To mark with kindled eye
How Taurus plunges up
  And Pegasus sweeps by,
  Wide-winged upon the sky!

Gravely I question him,
  My friend with curly coat:
"What think you of the stars
  That in the ether float —
  The Lion and the Goat,

"The Peacock and the Swan,
  The Little Dog, the Great?
Think you their light shall fail
  At any early date?"
  He yawns to say it's late!

Vainly I point him plain
  The Dog-Star following
His Master in the hunt
  Across the skies of spring —
  The Sword-Belt glittering.

My heedless terrier
  Cares not a fig for skies,

But stares at me with love's
　　Unchallenging surmise —
　　Twin stars within his eyes!

And leaps beneath my touch
　　As home from shore we steal,
While hunting overhead
　　I watch Orion wheel,
　　With Sirius at heel!
　　　　　　　　Agnes Kendrick Gray

THE LOOM

MY brother, the god, and I grow sick
Of heaven's heights.
We plunge to the valley to hear the tick
Of days and nights.
We walk and loiter around the Loom
To see, if we may,
The Hand that smashes the beam in the gloom
To the shuttle's play;
Who grows the wool, who cards and spins,
Who clips and ties;
For the storied weave of the Gobelins,
Who draughts and dyes.

But whether you stand or walk around
You shall but hear
A murmuring life, as it were the sound
Of bees or a sphere.
No Hand is seen, but still you may feel
A pulse in the thread,
And thought in every lever and wheel
Where the shuttle sped,

Dripping the colors, as crushed and urged —
Is it cochineal? —
Shot from the shuttle, woven and merged
A tale to reveal.
Woven and wound in a bolt and dried
As it were a plan.
Closer I looked at the thread and cried:
The thread is man!

Then my brother, curious, strong and bold,
Tugged hard at the bolt
Of the woven life; for a length unrolled
The cryptic cloth.
He gasped for labor, blind for the moult
Of the up-winged moth.
While I saw a growth and a mad crusade
That the Loom had made;
Land and water and living things,
Till I grew afraid
For mouths and claws and devil wings,
And fangs and stings,
And tiger faces with eyes of hell
In caves and holes.
And eyes in terror and terrible
For awakened souls.

I stood above my brother, the god,
Unwinding the roll,
And a tale came forth of the woven slain
Sequent and whole,
Of flint and bronze, trowel and hod,
The wheel and the plane,
The carven stone and the graven clod

Painted and baked.
And cromlechs, proving the human heart
Has always ached;
Till it puffed with blood and gave to art
The dream of the dome;
Till it broke and the blood shot up like fire
In tower and spire.

And here was the Persian, Jew and Goth
In the weave of the cloth;
Greek and Roman, Ghibelline, Guelph,
Angel and elf.
They were dyed in blood, tangled in dreams
Like a comet's streams.
And here were surfaces red and rough
In the finished stuff,
Where the knotted thread was proud and rebelled
As the shuttle proved
The fated warp and woof that held
When the shuttle moved;
And pressed the dye which ran to loss
In a deep maroon
Around an altar, oracle, cross
Or a crescent moon.
Around a face, a thought, a star
In a riot of war!
Then I said to my brother, the god, let be,
Though the thread be crushed,
And the living things in the tapestry
Be woven and hushed;
The Loom has a tale, you can see, to tell,
And a tale has told.
I love this Gobelin epical
Of scarlet and gold.

If the heart of a god may look with pride
At the wondrous weave,
It is something better to Hands which guide —
I see and believe.

Edgar Lee Masters

THE DEAR MYSTERY

Joy, and the triumph and the doom of gladness
Make in my breast a music sweet as sadness;
Shall I not sing for sorrow, and again
Cry out, for the sheer joyousness of pain!
For all life's moods go murmuring like strings
In a low chord, and all things sound all things,
Through alternations of the grave and glad:
Yet, in the end, all things are grave and sad.
I feel all things, but cannot comprehend;
And run, laughing and weeping, to the end
Of the dear mystery, the fated race —
And the deep darkness covers up my face.

John Hall Wheelock

LITTLE AND LONELY UNDER THE EVENING STAR

Little and lonely under the evening star —
These are the children of men that are wandering by,
Each with his packet of dreams and sandals of pain
Scarred by revolt and white with the dust of despair;
Gypsies of thorn-marked brows and blood-clotted hair,
All of them fated to dream what is ever vain,
Born unto song and sorrow, and marked to die,
Little as buttercups under the heel of June,
Little as wind-cries under the edge of the moon,

See — through the dusk of an hour they are wan-
    dering by,
These with the souls as vast as a God's dreams are —
Little and lonely under the evening star!

George Brandon Saul

THE WATER OF DIRCE

"If but the Gods, of their mercy,
  Would let me return ere I die,
To drink of the water of Dirce —
  On the cool sprinkled margin to lie!

"Yes, I drank of the Marcian waters,
  Of Bandusia's song-haunted spring;
But not though Mnemosyne's daughters
  The crystal of Helicon bring —

"Not they, not the charm-weaving Circe,
  Could make me forget or forego, —
I was used to the water of Dirce,
  I long for it, thirst for it so!

"The snows of Cithaeron have chilled it —
  I shall cease from this fever and pain,
If but the Gods have so willed it
  I taste that wild sweetness again!"

Then answered the Gods, of their mercy,
  "We give thee thy thirst and thy love,
But seek not the water of Dirce —
  For thy Youth was the sweetness thereof."

Edith M. Thomas

THIS IS THE SHAPE OF THE LEAF

THIS is the shape of the leaf, and this of the flower,
And this the pale bole of the tree
Which watches its bough in a pool of unwavering
    water
In a land we never shall see.

The thrush on the bough is silent, the dew falls softly,
In the evening is hardly a sound.
And the three beautiful pilgrims who come here to-
    gether
Touch lightly the dust of the ground,

Touch it with feet that trouble the dust but as wings
    do,
Come shyly together, are still,
Like dancers who wait, in a pause of the music, for
    music
The exquisite silence to fill.

This is the thought of the first, and this of the second,
And this the grave thought of the third:
'Linger we thus for a moment, palely expectant,
And silence will end, and the bird

'Sing the pure phrase, sweet phrase, clear phrase in
    the twilight
To fill the blue bell of the world;
And we, who on music so leaflike have drifted to-
    gether,
Leaflike apart shall be whirled

'Into what but the beauty of silence, silence forever?'

. . . This is the shape of the tree,
And the flower, and the leaf, and the three pale beau-
     tiful pilgrims;
This is what you are to me.

Conrad Aiken

Δώρια

Be in me as the eternal moods
          of the bleak wind, and not
As transient things are —
          gaiety of flowers.
Have me in the strong loneliness
          of sunless cliffs
And of grey waters.
          Let the gods speak softly of us
In days hereafter,
          The shadowy flowers of Orcus
Remember thee.

Ezra Pound

POPPIES

My words flash over you
and beat upon you
like crystal fringes of the rain
on the stately fire
of unquenchable poppies.

My words circle and search
and drink of you
as bronze, importunate bees
drink the bitter of dreams
from the fire cups
of indifferent poppies.

My words clasp and sing
and fold over you
as leaf darkness sinks
and folds on the proud scarlet
of imperial poppies.

Henry Bellamann

VISION

You who flutter and quiver
An instant
Just beyond my apprehension;
Lady,
I will find the white orchid for you,
If you will but give me
One smile between those wayward drifts of hair.

I will break the wild berries that loop themselves over
        the marsh-pool,
For your sake,
And the long green canes that swish against each other,
I will break, to set in your hands.
For there is no wonder like to you,
You who flutter and quiver
An instant
Just beyond my apprehension.

John Gould Fletcher

ORIENTALE

i spoke to thee
with a smile and thou didst not
answer
thy mouth is as
a chord of crimson music
                Come hither
O thou, is life not a smile?

i spoke to thee with
a song and thou
didst not listen
thine eyes are as a vase
of divine silence
> Come hither
O thou, is life not a song?

i spoke
to thee with a soul and
thou didst not wonder
thy face is as a dream locked
in white fragrance
> Come hither
O thou, is life not love?

i speak to
thee with a sword
and thou art silent
thy breast is as a tomb
softer than flowers
> Come hither
O thou, is love not death?
>> *E. E. Cummings*

IMPERATRIX

WHY have you come if for a moment only
Like dawn inviolate upon a hill?
Long with the need of you have I been lonely;
Now you will go and leave me lonelier still!
Cruel were my lips upon your mouth's keen gladness,
And fearful my soul betrayed in its unrest.
Oh you will go and leave me to my madness, —
And I had dreamed to fail against your breast!

Now is the distance looming dimmer and vaster
Between us, like dead suns in endless space.
Oh I shall run to meet my doom the faster
For all the stars (forgotten in your face)
That went down to imperial disaster,
Consumed in your imperial embrace!

Gustav Davidson

FAITH OF APPEARANCES

WHAT most is certain
Soonest goes —
The shining dream,
The cut rose,

The slanted sun,
The shapely fire.
All return,
But all retire;

And by another
It is said
These are false
And things are dead.

But nothing now
Of what we know —
Till we die —
Can ever go:

The second year
We saw the lawn,
After an ocean
Overgone;

The hasting home;
The world in love;
Then snow, and starving
Birds above;

The cruel sky;
The tender brain;
Thronging joy;
And lonely pain.

Only appearances
Are true —
While we live —
For me and you.

Mark Van Doren

LET NO CHARITABLE HOPE

Now let no charitable hope
Confuse my mind with images
Of eagle and of antelope:
I am in nature none of these.

I was, being human, born alone;
I am, being woman, hard beset;
I live by squeezing from a stone
The little nourishment I get.

In masks outrageous and austere
The years go by in single file;
But none has merited my fear,
And none has quite escaped my smile.

Elinor Wylie

TOWARD THE PIRÆUS

I

I LOVED you :
men have writ and women have said
they loved,
but as the Pythoness stands by the altar,
intense and may not move,

till the fumes pass over ;
and may not falter or break,
till the priest has caught the words
that mar or make
a deme or a ravaged town ;

so I, though my knees tremble,
my heart break,
must note the rumbling,
heed only the shuddering
down in the fissure beneath the rock
of the temple floor ;

must wait and watch
and may not turn nor move,
nor break from my trance to speak
so slight, so sweet,
so simple a word as love.

II

It was not chastity that made me cold nor fear,
only I knew that you, like myself, were sick
of the puny race that crawls and quibbles and lisps
of love and love and lovers and love's deceit.

It was not chastity that made me wild, but fear
that my weapon, tempered in different heat,
was over-matched by yours, and your hand
skilled to yield death-blows, might break

With the slightest turn — no ill will meant —
my own lesser, yet still somewhat fine-wrought,
fiery-tempered, delicate, over-passionate steel.

H. D.

DIVERSITY

You turn your eyes away, but still I have
The flash of startled horror that they threw,
Now you have found that love is wholly two
And there are chasms as final as a grave
Within its dreams.   But I shall not be sad
Beyond your sadness, always having asked
Meeting, not merging.   Sometimes mute and masked,
I knew that you were also, and was glad.

Something there is that keeps you close immured,
Sets you apart, so makes you visible;
Tear down the walls — you will be more obscured
And I forget to love you quite so well;
And you in time will not remember me
Who hurt you now with this diversity.

Frank Ernest Hill

THE DARK CHAMBER

The brain forgets but the blood will remember.
There, when the play of sense is over,
The last low spark in the darkest chamber
Will hold all there is of love and lover.

The war of words, the life-long quarrel
Of self against self will resolve into nothing;
Less than the chain of berry-red coral
Crying against the dead black of her clothing.

What has the brain that it hopes to last longer?
The blood will take from forgotten violence,
The groping, the break of her voice in anger.
There will be left only color and silence.

These will remain, these will go searching
Your veins for life when the flame of life smoulders:
The night that you two saw the mountains marching
Up against dawn with the stars on their shoulders —

The jetting poplars' arrested fountains
As you drew her under them, easing her pain —
The notes, not the words, of a half-finished sentence —
The music, the silence. . . . These will remain.

Louis Untermeyer

AUGUST NIGHT

On a midsummer night, on a night that was eerie with
    stars,
  In a wood too deep for a single star to look through,
You led down a path whose turnings you knew in the
    darkness,
    But the scent of the dew-dripping cedars was all
      that I knew.

I drank of the darkness, I was fed with the honey of
    fragrance,
    I was glad of my life, the drawing of breath was
      sweet;

I heard your voice, you said, "Look down, see the
    glow-worm!"
  It was there before me, a small star white at my
    feet.

We watched while it brightened as though it were
    breathed on and burning,
  This tiny creature moving over earth's floor —
"'*L'amor che move il sole e l'altre stelle.*'"
  You said, and no more.
Sara Teasdale

THE SWAMP

Love called me like a beacon on a hill,
With all the flickering odors of the dark,
And the sharp spurt of fireflies, spark on spark,
And beckoning glimmer of the window-sill;
Low like his arms the skyward branches came,
Outlined in down of flame.

I dug my face in leaves.   The hovering tree
Laid his swift hands on me,
His careless, thousand-fingered, merciful touch.
The wind that wearied him from side to side
Washed through me like a tide,
And led me past the taloned shadows' clutch
Where the slow swamp lies ambushed to the south.
My feet took hold on their accustomed trace.
And lo, at last I guessed Love's secret face
And the forbidden kisses of his mouth.

Like a cold knife lay on my throat the dew,
Leaves on my lids, and on my slackening heart
The silence, beating like another heart.
Less near and less the need of living grew.

The weary night dragged like a tale of years
Her tense, unresting planets overhead;
The keen grass murmured of the happy dead
That never know its rustling in their ears.
Through the desirous grass my will might seep
Delicious, irresponsible as tears.
Love, the great lover, my submission bore
Surely to some good ending, safe and deep;
Dead Love, that giveth his beloved sleep —
He that hath nothing better, nothing more.

Almost I slipped my hand in his to go;
When lo, a little dawn-wind like a child
Came singing, and the feathery rushes piled
Their plumes together singing.   To and fro
The gray veils of the cloistered moss bowed low
In endless adoration.   Lines of white,
On Gothic brambles truculent and wild
And roots like cunning carvings of delight,
Breathed out, because the very dawn had smiled
Seeing the miracle of the swamp in spring;
The morning like a legend long ago
Walked on the water, kindling ring on ring.

The water broke in irised arc and shoal —
Green snakes with touches exquisite and long,
More rhythmic than the fresh-of-morning song
The mocking-bird jets spattered from the brake.
Like some squat Eastern god, macabre, droll,
The alligator shot a silvery wake.
Small outcast creatures quavered into sight
Through elf-lock tangles of the lily-stem,
And pelted me with childish gifts of seeds
Until I noticed them,
The wonderful, the holy little weeds.

Gnats woke the air to fluting spray of gold.
The buzzard floated with an angel's flight
On motionless wide wings,
Effortless, not with any wind at strife. —
For God being God, who said, "Let there be Light,"
Cannot at all withhold
Some beauty from abominable things,
Some good from life, yes, even from my life.

Death called me like a beacon on a hill,
But smokily, as wood-fires dim and drowse
In sunshine when the early wind is still —
I lit the patient hearth-fire in the house.

Beatrice Ravenel

MARSH–GRASS

I saw the marsh-grass blowing;
    It took me far away;
For I was born where marsh-grass
    Was endlessly at play.

Its ripples were the gladdest things
    That one could ever see,
So who would think that marsh-grass
    Would bring the tears to me?

Jessie B. Rittenhouse

I KNOW THAT ANY WEED CAN TELL

I know that any weed can tell
    And any red leaf knows
That what is lost is found again
    To blossom in a rose.

The weakest is the strongest, too;
    For any moss has shown
How strong its frailest fingers are
    To split the biggest stone.

And so I go my quiet way
    As any quiet thing;
I know the weed and moss too well
    To be afraid to sing!

               Louis Ginsberg

THE TWO NESTS

THE wonder was on me in Curraghmacall,
    When I was as tall as the height of your knee,
That the wren should be building a hole in the wall
    Instead of a nest in a tree.

And I still do be thinking it strange, when I pass
    A pasture that has to be evenly ploughed,
That the lark should be building a hole in the grass
    Instead of a nest in a cloud.

               Francis Carlin

DE GUSTIBUS

ONE used his pinions eagle-like,
    And straight against the sun would rise
And scout among the stars, and strike
    His quarry from across the skies;

And one was as the bee that strives
    Against no wind, but simply blows
Across the garden, and arrives
    Upon an unsuspected rose.

               John Erskine

SCATHELESS

Lord, I am humbled by the great,
  For all the great have deadly foes;
There is a worm would like to eat
  The heart of every perfect rose;

There is a crow would like to pick
  The bones of every glory bare;
My enemies are gentle souls
  And for my death they do not care.

My enemies still suffer me
  And I am scatheless to this hour.
Men hunt upon the hills of time
  A nobler quarry to devour.

Marguerite Wilkinson

GOLDEN FALCON

He sees the circle of the world
  Alive with wings that he
Was born to rend; his eyes are stars
  Of amber cruelty.

God lit the fire in his eyes
  And bound swords on his feet,
God fanned the furnace of his heart
  To everlasting heat.

His two eyes take in all the sky,
  East, West, North, and South,
Opposite as poles they burn;
  And death is in his mouth.

Death because his Maker knew
  That death is last and best,
Because He gives to those He loves
  The benison of rest.

Golden, cruel word of God
  Written on the sky!
Living things are lovely things,
  And lovely things must die.
                    Robert P. Tristram Coffin

STANDARDS

WHITE is the skimming gull on the somber green of the
        fir-trees,
Black is the soaring gull on a snowy glimmer of cloud.
                    Charles Wharton Stork

THE CYCLE

The clapping blackness of the wings of pointed cor-
        morants, the great indolent planes
Of autumn pelicans nine or a dozen strung shorelong,
But chiefly the gulls, the cloud-caligraphers of windy
        spirals before a storm,
Cruise north and south over the sea-rocks and over
That bluish enormous opal; very lately these alone,
        these and the clouds
And westering lights of heaven, crossed it; but then
A hull with standing canvas crept about Point
        Lobos . . . now all day long the steamers
Smudge the opal's rim; often a seaplane troubles
The sea-wind with its throbbing heart. These will
        increase, the others diminish; and later
These will diminish; our Pacific have pastured

The Mediterranean torch and passed it west across the
        fountains of the morning;
And the following desolation that feeds on Crete
Feed here; the clapping blackness of the wings of
        pointed cormorants, the great sails
Of autumn pelicans, the gray sea-going gulls,
Alone will streak the enormous opal, the earth have
        peace like the broad water, our blood's
Unrest have doubled to Asia and be peopling
Europe again, or dropping colonies at the morning
        star: what moody traveler
Wanders back here, watches the sea-fowl circle
The old sea-granite and cemented granite with one
        regard, and greets my ghost,
One temper with the granite, bulking about here?

                         Robinson Jeffers

THE LOON

A LONELY lake, a lonely shore,
A lone pine leaning on the moon;
All night the water-beating wings
Of a solitary loon.

With mournful wail from dusk to dawn
He gibbered at the taunting stars —
A hermit soul gone raving mad,
And beating at his bars.

                         Lew Sarett

A SIDMOUTH SOUL

SALCOMBE HILL and three hills more
Lie to leftward of this shore.
On the right Peak Hill arises
Sickening, like the other four.

Two score rotting years I've seen
Sidmouth sit those hills between:
Only Sidmouth — and twice over
Must I bide it, as I've been.

Then a churchyard hole for me,
By the dull voice of the sea.
Rotting, still in Sidmouth rotting,
Rotting to eternity.

Cale Young Rice

THE TIDE

GOES in and out with its gigantic tread
The tide, a beast fastidious of its bed.
It waddles up like Behemoth, from the Deep,
To search the shelving shallows for its sleep,
Then with a trampling it draws back again . . .

It teems with hordes for watching fishermen
That wait about the cluttered wharves of the town
Or push out where the nets are studded down . . .

The pitchforked fish — obscene, white belly up —
Hurled out as worthless (that the gulls may sup
Screaming and wheeling in coveys) lard the drift.

The anchored boats against the current lift
Or lie side-cast on endless levels of sand;

The bay seems here begotten of the land,
The land — of sea and sky! . . . chaos spawns all!

Along the ooze primordial creatures sprawl:
Things carrying shells for house: blind lives that put
The body forth, transmuted to a foot;

Flanged, steel-blue sea-worms, ribbons that reach
    and draw;
Small monsters born of life's first groping law;
Embryons all eye, set drifting; creatures rare
That run like clocks in crystal; some, as fair
As beauty's perfect self, whose forms transgress
The general norm of primal ugliness,
Wave sapphire fringes, sail with shining sails,
'Sconce gleaming bodies in laced and exquisite grails.
For the old, blind slime again gets motion here
Where life's first efforts into being peer
Still, and where, naked and raw to wind and sun,
The ravels of the first creation run.

                           Harry Kemp

THE GROUNDSWELL

Marcia Funebre

With heavy doleful clamour, hour on hour, and day
    on day,
The muddy groundswell lifts and breaks and falls and
    slides away.

The cold and naked wind runs shivering over the
    sands,
Salt are its eyes, open its mouth, its brow wet, blue
    its hands.

It finds naught but a starving gull whose wings trail
    at its side,
And the dull battered wreckage, grey jetsam of the
    tide.

The lifeless chilly slaty sky with no blue hope is lit,
A rusty waddling steamer plants a smudge of smoke
    on it.

Stupidly stand the factory chimneys staring over all,
The grey grows ever denser, and soon the night will
fall :

The wind runs sobbing over the beach and touches
with its hands
Straw, chaff, old bottles, broken crates, the litter of
the sands.

Sometimes the bloated carcase of a dog or fish is
found,
Sometimes the rumpled feathers of a sea-gull shot or
drowned.

Last year it was an unknown man who came up from
the sea.
There is his grave hard by the dunes under a stunted
tree.

With heavy doleful clamour, hour on hour, and day
on day,
The muddy groundswell lifts and breaks and falls
and slides away.

John Gould Fletcher

WHALE

Rain, with a silver flail;
  Sun, with a golden ball;
Ocean, wherein the whale
  Swims minnow-small;
I heard the whale rejoice
  And cynic sharks attend;
He cried with a purple voice,
  "The Lord is my friend!"

"With flanged and battering tail,
  With huge and dark baleen,
He said, 'let there be whale
  In the Cold and Green!'

"He gave me a water spout,
  A side like a harbor wall;
The Lord from cloud looked out
  And planned it all.

"With glittering crown atilt
  He leaned on a glittering rail;
He said, 'Where sky is spilt,
  Let there be Whale.'

"Tier upon tier of wings
  Blushed and blanched and bowed;
Phalanxed fiery things
  Cried in the cloud;

"Million-eyed was the mirk
  At the plan not understood;
But the Lord looked on his work
  And saw it was good.

"He gave me marvelous girth
  For the curve of back and breast,
And a tiny eye of mirth
  To hide His jest.

"He made me a floating hill,
  A plunging deep-sea mine.
This was the Lord's will;
  The Lord is divine.

"I magnify His name
  In earthquake and eclipse,
In weltering molten flame
  And wrecks of ships,

"In waves that lick the moon;
  I, the plough of the sea!
I am the Lord's boon,
  The Lord made me!"

The sharks barked from beneath,
  As the great whale rollicked and roared,
"Yes, and our grinning teeth,
  Was it not the Lord?"

Then question pattered like hail
  From fishes large and small.
"The Lord is mighty," said Whale,
  The Lord made all!

"His is a mammoth jest
  Life never may betray;
He has laid it up in His breast
  Till Judgment Day;

"But high when combers foam
  And tower their last of all,
My power shall haul you home
  Through Heaven wall.

"A trumpet then in the gates,
  To the ramps a thundering drum,
I shall lead you where He waits
  For His Whale to come.

"Where His cloudy seat is placed
   On high in an empty dome,
I shall trail the Ocean abased
   In chains of foam,

"Unwieldy, squattering dread;
   Where the blazing cohorts stand
At last I shall lift my head
   As it feels His hand.

"Then wings with a million eyes
   Before mine eyes shall quail:
'Look you, all Paradise,
   I was His Whale!'"

I heard the Whale rejoice,
   As he splayed the waves to a fan;
"And the Lord shall say with His Voice,
   '*Leviathan!*'

"The Lord shall say with His Tongue,
   'Now let all Heaven give hail
To my Jest when I was young,
   To my very Whale!'"

Then the Whale careered in the Sea,
   He floundered with flailing tail;
Flourished and rollicked he,
   "Aha!   Mine Empery!
For the Lord said, 'Let Whale be!'
   And there was Whale!"

William Rose Benét

SEA BORN

My mother bore me in an island town,
So I love windy water and the sight
Of luggers sailing by in thin moonlight —
I wear the sea as others wear a crown!
My mother bore me near the spinning water,
Water was the first sound upon my ears,
And near the sea her mother bore her daughter,
Close to a window looking on the weirs.
Ever a wind is moaning where I go,
I never stand at night upon a quay
But I must strain my eyes for sails that blow,
But I must strain my ears to hear the sea.
My mother bore me in a seaport town,
I wear the sea as others wear a crown!

Harold Vinal

THE GREAT SEDUCER

Who looks too long from his window
At the grey, wide, cold sea,
Where breakers scour the beaches
With fingers of sharp foam;
Who looks too long through the grey pane
At the mad, wild, bold sea,
Shall sell his hearth to a stranger
And turn his back on home.

Who looks too long from his window —
Though his wife waits by the fireside —
At a ship's wings in the offing,
At a gull's wings on air,
Shall latch his gate behind him,

Though his cattle call from the byre-side,
And kiss his wife — and leave her —
And wander everywhere.

Who looks too long in the twilight,
Or the dawn-light, or the noon-light,
Who sees an anchor lifted
And hungers past content,
Shall pack his chest for the world's end,
For alien sun, or moonlight,
And follow the wind, sateless —
To Disillusionment!

Cale Young Rice

COMPLIMENT TO MARINERS

Man's earthliness which saints deplore
Suggests that his most potent worth
Is surely to refresh the store
Of diligent dead, compact with earth.

In their dull drudgery he shall
Enlist, save that he makes his tomb
The sea where pallid fishes fall
Like slow snow down the tall green gloom.

Such proud exemption justly goes
Never to them who vainly sing
In strenuous awe before a rose,
Or tremble in the furious spring.

Wherefore, dark mariners, you earn
A certain envy that you set
Wide banners on the wind, and spurn
The crowded island, and forget

You ever trod its greenest shore;
But most, that finally you stand
In cold unlaboring coral or
Insinuate the sterile sand.

George H. Dillon

DIVERS

CLAD in thick mail he stumbles down the floor
  Of the dark primaeval ocean; — on his head
  A casque more gross than ever helmeted
Crusader against Saracen.   Before
His glass-dimmed eyes dart shapes like fiends of yore,
  Or like malignant spirits of the dead,
  To snatch and snap the line where through is fed
A meagre air to that strange visitor.
Stumbling we grope and stifle here below
  In the gross garb of this too cumbering flesh,
    And draw such hard-won breaths as may be drawn,
Until, perchance with pearls, we rise and go
  To doff our diver's mail and taste the fresh,
    The generous winds of the eternal dawn.

Robert Haven Schauffler

WHO GOES BY

WHO goes by like the tread of armies, all that have
      marched since the world began,
Hordes of the Hun and the vagrant Vandal, hosts of
      Timur and Genghis Khan?

Who goes by with the voice of thunder, lilting in
      triumph a titan tune,
Reeling the stars in their wheeling courses, rocking
      the disk of the rising moon?

Who goes by like the sound of surges heard on the
    Hebridean shore,
Or where the ice-packs grind and sunder, off the verges
    of Labrador?

Who goes by like the avalanches at the hands of the
    sun set free?
Who goes by like the draught of forges under Aetna
    or Stromboli?

Who goes by at the tide of the Lion as with the wings
    of the tempest shod?
Who but the wind that is God's evangel, setting his
    lips to the trump of God!

Clinton Scollard

SONG OF THE FULL CATCH

HERE's good wind, here's sweet wind,
Here's good wind and my woman calls me!
Straight she stands there by the pine-tree,
Faithful waits she by the cedar,
She will smile and reach her hands
When she sees my thousand salmon!
Here's good wind and my woman calls me.

Here's clear water, here's swift water,
Here's bright water and my woman waits me!
She will call me from the sea's mouth.
Sweet her pine-bed when the morning
Lights my canoe and the river ends.
Here's good wind, here's swift water,
Strong as love when my woman calls me!

Constance Lindsay Skinner

MY JEWELS

I have seen the swelling sun,
Like a blood-filled bubble, fall
To the sharpened world, and burst on the tip
Of a pine tree that is tall.

I have seen a clear, glass cloud,
Painted with pink and with gray,
Float to the top of the tilted gold cup
Of the dawn, and spill away.

I have heard a woodpecker
Beating the heart of a tree,
And I have kissed naked young leaves that stretched
Cold washed faces up to me.

Mary Dixon Thayer

PROPOSED BARTER

For one New England pinewood on a hill,
Ringed with tall birches peering whitely in,
Where only mushrooms know how to stand still,
So buoyant is the brown-gold air, so thin
The pretext for mere stillness (how much more
The birches like their tiptoe life! how wild
The halfgrown pinetree like a romping child!)
For one sheep-pasture with a nibbled floor
Of green-gray turf where puff-balls gleam like nails,
For sweet-briar wands much traveled by blue snails
And sweet-briar bloom much loitered in by bees,
For goldenrod along a twisted lane, —
Give me a tawny country without trees,
That runs to cactus through transparent miles.
Give me the rhythm of a wilful plain
Frosted with alkali like silver salt,

That wants its own way, scorning change of seasons
Unless to let the prickly-pear try out
Its brusque idea of flowering, curious styles
In color or design : or for good reasons
To let the marching April yucca halt
And dream within its ivory tower all day.
Give me sharp mountain rims that have no doubt
Of their own sapphire armor, shield and spear.
Give me that salamander in the red dust.
Never ask why.   How could I make it clear?
I knew all these : hunger for them I must.
White thistle-poppies at the canyon-mouth
Recur : and I would live where through the year
The spiked *biznaga* leans always a little south.

Grace Hazard Conkling

THE STRANGER

I HEDGE rebellious grasses in,
But where shall ownership begin?

The spider spins her silvery bars
Between me and the cosmos' stars,

And ere I waken is astir
To write revolt in gossamer!

With beady and foreboding eye
The turtle peers as I go by :

The shell that shuts him in is stout —
Stronger the code that shuts me out!

What dauntless and primeval stock
Makes yonder stone its council-rock?

What old, indomitable breed
Takes this low bush for Runnymede?

Races whose titles run from God
Dispute my warrant to the sod!

I am Intrusion!   I am Danger!
Familiar, but for aye — the Stranger!
Daniel Henderson

A YOKE OF STEERS

A HEAVE of mighty shoulders to the yoke,
Square, patient heads, and flaring sweep of horn;
The darkness swirling down beneath their feet
Where sleeping valleys stir, and feel the dawn;
Uncouth and primal, on and up they sway,
Taking the summit in a drench of day.
The night-winds volley upward bitter-sweet,
And the dew shatters to a rainbow spray
Under the slow-moving, cloven feet.

There is a power here that grips the mind;
A force repressed and inarticulate,
Slow as the swing of centuries, as blind
As destiny, and as deliberate.

They will arrive in their appointed hour
Unhurried by the goad of lesser wills,
Bearing vast burdens on.
                          They are the great
Unconquerable spirit of these hills.
Du Bose Heyward

THE BRONCHO THAT WOULD NOT BE BROKEN

A LITTLE colt — broncho, loaned to the farm
To be broken in time without fury or harm,
Yet black crows flew past you, shouting alarm,
Calling, "Beware," with lugubrious singing. . . .
The butterflies there in the bush were romancing,
The smell of the grass caught your soul in a trance,
So why be a-fearing the spurs and the traces,
O broncho that would not be broken of dancing?

You were born with the pride of the lords great and
        olden
Who danced, through the ages, in corridors golden.
In all the wide farm-place the person most human.
You spoke out so plainly with squealing and capering,
With whinnying, snorting, contorting and prancing,
As you dodged your pursuers, looking askance,
With Greek-footed figures, and Parthenon paces,
O broncho that would not be broken of dancing.

The grasshoppers cheered   "Keep whirling," they
        said.
The insolent sparrows called from the shed
"If men will not laugh, make them wish they were
        dead."
But arch were your thoughts, all malice displacing,
Though the horse-killers came, with snake-whips
        advancing.
You bantered and cantered away your last chance,
And they scourged you, with Hell in their speech and
        their faces,
O broncho that would not be broken of dancing.

"Nobody cares for you," rattled the crows,
As you dragged the whole reaper, next day, down the
rows.
The three mules held back, yet you danced on your
toes.
You pulled like a racer, and kept the mules chasing.
You tangled the harness with bright eyes side-
glancing,
While the drunk driver bled you — a pole for a
lance —
And the giant mules bit at you — keeping their places.
O broncho that would not be broken of dancing.

In that last afternoon your boyish heart broke.
The hot wind came down like a sledge-hammer stroke.
The blood-sucking flies to a rare feast awoke.
And they searched out your wounds, your death-
warrant tracing.
And the merciful men, their religion enhancing,
Stopped the red reaper, to give you a chance.
Then you died on the prairie, and scorned all disgraces,
O broncho that would not be broken of dancing.

Vachel Lindsay

A TARTAR HORSE

His hooves kicked up the saffron dust
    From Isfahan to Tartary,
And golden bits as red as rust
    Could never bring him to his knee.

By bleaching desert paths where once
    The bearded Khan in splendor rode
He hears the whinney of response
    From phantom steeds that spurned the goad.

And racing with the racing wind
 Through careous rock across the plain
He feels the ghostly whips behind
 And yellow fingers in his mane.

When stopping short he lifts his head
 And, quivering-nostrilled, shrilly cries,
He turns upon a world that's dead
 The burning cities in his eyes.
Herbert Gorman

ON THE PASSING OF THE LAST FIRE HORSE FROM MANHATTAN ISLAND

I REMEMBER the cleared streets, the strange suspense
 As if a thunder-storm were under way;
Magnificently furious, hurrying thence
 The fire-eyed horses racing to the fray;
Out of old Homer where the heroes are,
 Beating upon the whirlwind thunderous hoofs,
Wild horses and plumed Ajax in his car:
 Oh, in those days we still possest the proofs
Men battled shouting by the gates of Troy,
 With shields of triple brass and spears of flame.
With what distended nostrils, what fierce joy,
 What ring on stone and steel those horses came!
Like horses of gods that whirl to the dawn's burning,
 They came, and they are gone, and unreturning.
Kenneth Slade Alling

THREE O'CLOCK

Morning

THE jewel-blue electric flowers
Are cold upon their iron trees.
Upraised, the deadly harp of rails

Whines for its interval of ease.
The stones keep all their daily speech
Buried, but can no more forget
Than would a water-vacant beach
The hour when it was wet.

A whitened few wane out like moons,
Ghastly from some torn edge of shade;
A drowning one, a reeling one,
And one still loitering after trade.
On high the candor of a clock
Portions the dark with solemn sound.
The burden of the bitten rock
Moans up from underground.

Far down the street a shutting door
Echoes the yesterday that fled
Among the days that should have been
Which people cities of the dead.
The banners of the steam unfold
Upon the towers to meet the day;
The lights go out in red and gold,
But time goes out in gray.

Ridgely Torrence

THE DRUG CLERK

THE drug clerk stands behind the counter
Young and dapper, debonair. . . .

Before him burn the great unwinking lights,
The hectic stars of city nights,
Red as hell's pit, green as a mermaid's hair.
A queer half-acrid smell is in the air.

Behind him on the shelves in ordered rows
With strange, abbreviated names
Dwell half the facts of life. That young man knows,
Bottled and boxed and powdered here,
Dumb tragedies, deceptions, secret shames,
And comedy, and fear.

Sleep slumbers here, like a great quiet sea
Shrunk to this bottle's compass, sleep that brings
Sweet respite from the teeth of pain
To those poor tossing things
That the white nurses watch so thoughtfully.
And here again
Dwell the shy souls of Maytime flowers
That shall make sweeter still those poignant hours
When wide-eyed youth looks on the face of love.
And, for those others who have found too late
The bitter fruits thereof,
Here are cosmetics, powders, paints, — the arts
That hunted women use to hunt again
With scented flesh for bait.
And here is comfort for the hearts
Of sucking babes in their first teething pain.
Here dwells the substance of huge fervid dreams,
Fantastic, many-colored, shot with gleams
Of ecstasy and madness, that shall come
To some pale, twitching sleeper in a bunk.
And here is courage, cheaply bought
To cure a sick blue funk,
And dearly paid for in the final sum.
Here in this powdered fly is caught
Desire more ravishing than Tarquin's, rape
And bloody-handed murder. And at last
When the one weary hope is past

Here is the sole escape,
The little postern in the house of breath
Where pallid fugitives keep tryst with death.

All this the drug clerk knows and there he stands,
Young and dapper, debonair. . . .
He rests a pair of slender hands,
Much manicured, upon the counter there
And speaks: "No, we don't carry no pomade.
We only cater to the high-class trade."

Eunice Tietjens

IN NEW YORK

I HAVE a need of silence and of stars;
Too much is said too loudly; I am dazed.
The silken sound of whirled infinity
Is lost in voices shouting to be heard.
I once knew men as earnest and less shrill.
An undermeaning that I caught, I miss
Among these ears that hear all sounds save silence,
These eyes that see so much but not the sky,
These minds that gain all knowledge but no calm.
If suddenly the desperate music ceased,
Could they return to life? or would they stand
In dancers' attitudes, puzzled, polite,
And striking vaguely hand on tired hand
For an encore, to fill the ghastly pause?
I do not know. Some rhythm there may be
I cannot hear. But I — oh, I must go
Back where the breakers of deep sunlight roll
Across flat fields that love and touch the sky;
Back to the more of earth, the less of man,
Where there is still a plain simplicity,

And friendship, poor in everything but love,
And faith, unwise, unquestioned, but a star.
Soon now the peace of summer will be there
With cloudy fire of myrtles in full bloom;
And, when the marvelous wide evenings come,
Across the molten river one can see
The misty willow-green of Arcady.
And then — the summer stars . . . I will go home.

William Alexander Percy

DUSK

THEY tell me she is beautiful, my City,
That she is colorful and quaint, alone
Among the cities.   But I, I who have known
Her tenderness, her courage, and her pity,
Have felt her forces mould me, mind and bone,
Life after life, up from her first beginning.
How can I think of her in wood and stone!
To others she has given of her beauty,
Her gardens, and her dim, old, faded ways,
Her laughter, and her happy, drifting hours,
Glad, spendthrift April, squandering her flowers,
The sharp, still wonder of her Autumn days;
Her chimes that shimmer from St. Michael's steeple
Across the deep maturity of June,
Like sunlight slanting over open water
Under a high, blue, listless afternoon.
But when the dusk is deep upon the harbor,
She finds *me* where her rivers meet and speak,
And while the constellations ride the silence
High overhead, her cheek is on my cheek.
I know her in the thrill behind the dark
When sleep brims all her silent thoroughfares.

She is the glamor in the quiet park
That kindles simple things like grass and trees,
Wistful and wanton as her sea-born airs,
Bringer of dim, rich, age-old memories.
Out on the gloom-deep water, when the nights
Are choked with fog, and perilous, and blind,
She is the faith that tends the calling lights.
Hers is the stifled voice of harbor bells
Muffled and broken by the mist and wind.
Hers are the eyes through which I look on life
And find it brave and splendid.   And the stir
Of hidden music shaping all my songs,
And these my songs, my all, belong to her.

                                  Du Bose Heyward

SANTA BARBARA BEACH

Now while the sunset offers,
Shall we not take our own:
The gems, the blazing coffers,
The seas, the shores, the throne?

The sky-ships, radiant-masted
Move out, bear low our way.
Oh, Life was dark while it lasted,
Now for enduring day.

Now with the world far under,
To draw up drowning men
And show them lands of wonder
Where they may build again.

There earthly sorrow falters,
There longing has its wage;

There gleam the ivory altars
Of our lost pilgrimage.

— Swift flame — then shipwrecks only
Beach in the ruined light;
Above them reach up lonely
The headlands of the night.

A hurt bird cries and flutters
Her dabbled breast of brown;
The western wall unshutters
To fling one last rose down.

A rose, a wild light after —
And life calls through the years,
"Who dreams my fountain's laughter,
Shall feed my wells with tears."

Ridgely Torrence

NEW ORLEANS

Do you remember
Honey-melon moon
Dripping thick sweet light
Where Canal Street saunters off by herself among
    quiet trees?
And the faint decayed patchouli —
Fragrance of New Orleans. . . .
New Orleans,
Like a dead tube rose
Upheld in the warm air. . . .
Miraculously whole.

Lola Ridge

NO ONE KNOWS THE COUNTRYSIDE

Last night I heard the eager rain
Busy in the leaves again;
Heard the plane-trees rise and break
The long summer sleep they make;
And O my heart was wide awake
And lonely for a northern lane.

For the lucid wet clear whistle
Of partridges in wheat and thistle,
And the dripping following sense
Of fog along a twisted fence,
Where, in soundless intervals,
Sudden muffled farmhouse walls,
Barns, and hooded ricks, and smells
Of smoke and hay and animals,
Step from the shadows and step back,
Into the white encircling wrack.
And then, hushed vacancy again,
A gradual lifting of the rain,
And trees on either side whose height
Brings that strange five-o-clock delight
Of mist and earth and solitude
That clings about a northern wood.

No one knows the countryside,
Deep and green and sweet and wide,
Unless on some soft gusty day
He has gone over, and far away
Crossed a ridge above a hill,
Along a little road, until,
Passing a little stream and mill,

All down under in the valleys,
He tramps the red damp forest alleys.
No one knows the countryside
Unless he's seen it in October,
When all the green has changed to fire
And all the gold is brown and sober,
And squirrels disturb the breathless gray
With tiny steps that die away.

Last night I heard the eager rain,
And I said to myself, I will rise and go,
For I am sick of this languid sea
And these naked plane-trees row on row,
And I'll go back where clouds uptost
Sing to the swaying bow of frost.
I who have known the passionate north,
Can I abide the fluent south?
For northern people do not speak
All day and night and all the week,
They do not gather in a crowd
And tell their secret thoughts aloud,
And so by keeping thus their peace,
The measures of their hearts increase.

I want again, with old persistence,
Northern horizons and distance,
Northern people, staid and kind,
Reading, where a northern blind,
Drawn, has shut the evening out
And brought a mellowness about.
I want a place of lamps and fires,
Of silence till some reader tires,
And then the knocking out of pipes,

A smile on casual northern lips,
A pleasant sleepy northern yawn,
And heavy northern sleep till dawn.
Where is the smell I used to know
Of leathered books and chintz and logs,
And roses in a china bowl, and slightly wet and snor-
  ing dogs,
And heavy rugs and shining floors,
And leafy dampness out of doors?

A little moon, engraved and thin,
A most enchanted autumn moon,
Is caught, an amber javelin,
In the dark heraldry of oaks;
And acridly chrysanthemums,
And acridly the burning mould,
Send up the incense of their fumes
In the blue twilight growing cold.
And all about there is a feeling
Of hearths, elate, sedate, appealing.
The moles are making warm their nests,
The rabbit's fur is growing whiter,
The owls put feathers on their breasts,
The chipmunks pack their granaries tighter,
And men chop logs and pile them high,
And watch the shifting northern sky.

Small wonder northern peoples have
A word no southern peoples know,
How can you have a home unless
You have the winter and the snow?
How capture this ingrained elation
Save with the year's slow full rotation?

And how can anybody tell
What is "within" and what "without,"
Unless there is the parable
Of tangible doors that really shut?
Poor Greeks, they saw "the wine dark sea,"
They had an adjective or so,
But all the terms, expressed or not,
Of northern folk they did not know;
The lovely, wistful, actual charms
That conjure walls and hearths and farms.

No one knows the countryside,
Sweet and deep and amplified,
Until he's watched it day by day,
Month by month, from frost to hay.
First the bare and breathing earth,
Then the tenuous shy birth,
Then the color in the hedges,
In the furrows, on the sedges;
Then the streams, released and quick,
Then the shadows, warm and thick,
Then the grain, invincible,
Then the drowsy lingering spell,
Water running quietly,
Willows weaving tapestry,
And then — a silence like a horn —
And the great encampments of the corn.

There are so many fools about,
God knows why God has made so many,
When, if he exercised his right,
There'd be so few, in fact, not any,
And of the fools who ring their bells
And fill the roads with contraband,

There are no fools whose itch is worse
Than those who hate their native land.
No witling, be it man or maid,
Who leaves one more for man afraid.

I know, and so do all of us,
That we — our breed — is filled with folly,
If I regarded only this
I too would drown in melancholy.
I know our leaders are absurd,
When not dishonest and corrupt,
I think reformers take our woes
And add to them until they're cupped,
Then hand to us their brimming drink
To watch, as sadists, how we shrink.
I think the small queer men who try
To end the mystery of wine,
Create a laughter in the sky
That some day they will find divine.
I'm sure no nation ever stormed
The gates of truth so ill-informed.
I know. . . . But, ah, I've heard the horn
That blows in autumn with the corn!
I know a hundred russet secrets,
And tawny truths and shimmering words;
I know the lifting mist of hills,
The thrifty valleys filled with birds;
I have gone up and down the ways
Where the high-headed mountains gaze.

No one knows the countryside,
Deep and green and sweetly wide,
Until he loves it as a woman,
Something warm and dear and human.

Struthers Burt

MY LAND

Not for long can I be angry with the most beautiful —
I look out of my vengefulness, and see her so young,
       so vastly young,
Wandering her fields beside Huron,
Or peering over Mt. Rainier.

Is she in daisies up to her knees?
Do I see that fresh white smile of hers in the morning-
       shadowed city?
Is this she clinging to the headlight of the locomotive
       that roars between the pine-lone mountains?
Are her ankles in the wash of sea-weed beside the sea-
       battered rocks?

Ah! never the curve of a hill but she has just gone
       beyond it,
And the prairies are as sweet with her as with clover
       and sage.
Her young breasts are soft against willow-leaves,
Her hands are quicker than birds in the vagueness of
       the forest.

Whether it is a dream that I have honey-gathered
       from the years of my days,
Whether it is so, and no dream,
I cannot help the love that goes out of me to these
       plains and hills,
These coasts, these cities, and these seas.

                           James Oppenheim

MOUNTAIN NIGHT

THESE mountains are too tall; these crags too starkly
    loom.
They will not clothe our shivering souls as cities must.
We walk through moonlit paths to forest-hidden
    doom.
These spires that spike the sky, we cannot bear their
    thrust.

The distant horses' bells ring pale as tepee smoke;
And women's laughter tinkles thin and strangely
    shrill.
The wraith-like moon now wears a mountain like a
    cloak.
Oh, city noises, break! The world is all too still!

Ralph Cheyney

THE PANTHER

THE moon shears up on Tahoe now;
The panther leaps to the tamarack bough.
She crouches, hugging the crooked limb;
She hears the nearing steps of him
Who sent the little puff of smoke
That stretched her mate beneath the oak.

Her eyes burn beryl, two yellow balls,
As Fate counts out his last footfalls.
A sudden spring, a demon cry,
Carnivorous laughter to the sky.
Her teeth are fastened in his throat
(The moon rides in her silver boat)
And now one scream of long delight
Across the caverns of the night!

Edwin Markham

FEUD

POOR wayworn creature! O sorely harried deer,
What drove you, quivering like a poplar-blade,
To refuge with my herd? What holds you here
Within my meadow, broken and afraid?

Tilting your nose to tainted air, you thrill
And freeze to wailing wolves! Fear you the sound
Of the coyotes eager for a tender kill?
Or yet the baying of the hunter's hound?

Let fall your anguish, harried one, and rest;
Bed yourself down among your kin, my cattle;
Sleep unperturbed, no spoiler shall molest
You here this night, for I shall wage your battle.

There was a day when coyotes in a pack,
Wolves of another hue, another breed,
With Christ upon their lips, set out to track
Me down and drop me, for my blood, my creed.

O hunted creature, once I knew the thud
Of padded feet that put you into flight,
The bugle-cry, suffused with lust for blood,
That trembled in the brazen bell of night.

I knew your frenzied rocky run, the burst
Of lungs, the rivers of fire in every vein;
I knew your foaming lip, your boundless thirst,
The rain of molten-hammering in your brain.

Bide with me then, against the wolves' return,
For I shall carry on the feud for you;
And it shall be, to me, of small concern
If the wolf-hearts walk on four soft feet or two.

Oh, let them come! And I shall burn their flanks
With a blast of hell to end their revelry,
And whistle molten silver through their ranks,
Laughing — one round for you and one for me.

Lew Sarett

THE BALLAD OF WILLIAM SYCAMORE

My father, he was a mountaineer,
His fist was a knotty hammer;
He was quick on his feet as a running deer,
And he spoke with a Yankee stammer.

My mother, she was merry and brave,
And so she came to her labor,
With a tall green fir for her doctor grave
And a stream for her comforting neighbor.

And some are wrapped in the linen fine,
And some like a godling's scion;
But I was cradled on twigs of pine
In the skin of a mountain lion.

And some remember a white, starched lap
And a ewer with silver handles;
But I remember a coonskin cap
And the smell of bayberry candles.

The cabin logs, with the bark still rough,
And my mother who laughed at trifles,
And the tall, lank visitors, brown as snuff,
With their long, straight squirrel-rifles.

I can hear them dance, like a foggy song,
Through the deepest one of my slumbers,
The fiddle squeaking the boots along
And my father calling the numbers.

The quick feet shaking the puncheon-floor,
And the fiddle squealing and squealing,
Till the dried herbs rattled above the door
And the dust went up to the ceiling.

There are children lucky from dawn till dusk,
But never a child so lucky!
For I cut my teeth on "Money Musk"
In the Bloody Ground of Kentucky!

When I grew tall as the Indian corn,
My father had little to lend me,
But he gave me his great, old powder-horn
And his woodsman's skill to befriend me.

With a leather shirt to cover my back,
And a redskin nose to unravel
Each forest sign, I carried my pack
As far as a scout could travel.

Till I lost my boyhood and found my wife,
A girl like a Salem clipper!
A woman straight as a hunting knife
With eyes as bright as the Dipper!

We cleared our camp where the buffalc feed,
Unheard-of streams were our flagons;
And I sowed my sons like the apple-seed
On the trail of the Western wagons.

They were right, tight boys, never sulky or slow,
A fruitful, a goodly muster.
The eldest died at the Alamo.
The youngest fell with Custer.

The letter that told it burned my hand.
Yet we smiled and said, "So be it!"
But I could not live when they fenced the land,
For it broke my heart to see it.

I saddled a red, unbroken colt
And rode him into the day there;
And he threw me down like a thunderbolt
And rolled on me as I lay there.

The hunter's whistle hummed in my ear
As the city-men tried to move me,
And I died in my boots like a pioneer
With the whole wide sky above me.

Now I lie in the heart of the fat, black soil,
Like the seed of a prairie-thistle;
It has washed my bones with honey and oil
And picked them clean as a whistle.

And my youth returns, like the rains of Spring,
And my sons, like the wild-geese flying;
And I lie and hear the meadow-lark sing
And have much content in my dying.

Go play with the towns you have built of blocks,
The towns where you would have bound me!
I sleep in my earth like a tired fox,
And my buffalo have found me.

Stephen Vincent Benét

SWEETGRASS RANGE

Come sell your pony, cowboy —
  Sell your pony to me;
Braided bridle and your puncher saddle,
  And spend your money free.

"If I should sell my pony,
  And ride the range no more,
Nail up my hat and my silver spurs
  Above my shanty door;

"And let my door stand open wide
  To the snow and the rain and sun;
And bury me under the green sweetgrass
  Where you hear the river run."

As I came down the sweetgrass range
  And by the cabin door,
I heard a singing in the early dusk
  Along the river shore;

I heard a singing to the early stars,
  And the tune of a pony's feet.
The joy of the riding singer
  I never shall forget.
                              Edwin Ford Piper

IN THE PASS

At Beckwith in the pass below Chilcoot
The wind set Pan-pursed lips as to a flute,
And blew a poignant long autumnal strain
That brought the rain.

And all the little streams that cut the clay
Made in their joy a bubbling roundelay;
The glinting rabbit-brush through the gray blur
Grew yellower.

The cattle lifted heads and drank the mist;
The billowing mountains swam in amethyst;
And there were bursts of laughter from the grass
Throughout the pass.

Those who had known the parching dread of drouth
Had praise for answered prayer upon the mouth;
And those who had faced famine and feared fire
Had their desire.

Clinton Scollard

A DANCE FOR RAIN

You may never see rain, unless you see
A dance for rain at Cochiti,
Never hear thunder in the air
Unless you hear the thunder there,
Nor know the lightning in the sky
If there's no pole to know it by . . .
They dipped the pole just as I came,
And I can never be the same
Since those feathers gave my brow
The touch of wind that's on it now,
Bringing over the arid lands
Butterfly gestures from Hopi hands
And holding me, till earth shall fail,
As close to earth as a fox's tail.

I saw them, naked, dance in line
Before the candles of a leafy shrine;

Before a saint in a Christian dress
I saw them dance their holiness,
I saw them reminding him all day long
That death is weak and life is strong
And urging the fertile earth to yield
Seed from the loin and seed from the field.
A feather in the hair and a shell at the throat
Were lifting and falling with every note
Of the chorus-voices and the drum,
Calling for the rain to come.
A fox on the back, and shaken on the thigh
Rain-cloth woven from the sky,
And under the knee a turtle-rattle
Clacking with the toes of sheep and cattle —
These were the men, their bodies painted
Earthen, with a white rain slanted;
These were the men, a windy line,
Their elbows green with a growth of pine.
And in among them, close and slow,
Women moved the way things grow,
With a mesa-tablet on the head
And a little grassy creeping tread
And with sprays of pine moved back and forth,
While the dance of the men blew from the north,
Blew from the south and east and west
Over the field and over the breast.
And the heart was beating in the drum,
Beating for the rain to come.

Dead men out of earlier lives,
Leaving their graves, leaving their wives,
Were partly flesh and partly clay,
And their heads were corn that was dry and gray.

They were ghosts of men and once again
They were dancing like a ghost of rain;
For the spirits of men, the more they eat,
Have happier hands and lighter feet,
And the better they dance the better they know
How to make corn and children grow.

And so in Cochiti that day
They slowly put the sun away
And they made a cloud and they made it break
And they made it rain for the children's sake.
And they never stopped the song or the drum
Pounding for the rain to come.

The rain made many suns to shine,
Golden bodies in a line
With leaping feather and swaying pine.
And the brighter the bodies, the brighter the rain
As thunder heaped it on the plain.
Arroyos had been empty, dry,
But now were running with the sky;
And the dancers' feet were in a lake,
Dancing for the people's sake.
And the hands of a ghost had made a cup
For scooping handfuls of water up;
And he poured it into a ghostly throat,
And he leaped and waved with every note
Of the dancers' feet and the songs of the drum
That had called the rain and made it come.

For this was not a god of wood,
This was a god whose touch was good,
You could lie down in him and roll
And wet your body and wet your soul;

For this was not a god in a book,
This was a god that you tasted and took
Into a cup that you made with your hands,
Into your children and into your lands —
This was a god that you could see,
Rain, rain in Cochiti!

Witter Bynner

ENTRY TO THE DESERT

If I should hasten or cry out,
I would not see the aspens whipping on the rim
Of the red butte to the north;
I would not hear
The rainy march of the wind that breathes
A deeper shadow on the corn.

So let me no less delicately plant
My footsteps on this desert earth
Than the prim quail that leads her grave procession
        through the sage,
Or the gray rabbit, pausing lop-eared and alert,
Scenting the rain.

James Rorty

WHERE NO SEEDS GROW

Here rest no homes, here grow no seeds,
Here come no laborers to toil:
Alone along the stretch of soil
The boulders cluster, and the weeds.
And barrenly, and worm defiled,
These acres waste, with such a blight
As he who never dared to fight . . .
Or she who never bore a child.

Dorothy Dow

THE DESERT REMEMBERS HER REASONS

How many rivers swerved aside
Rather than take a stony bride!
Rather than take a stony bride
Rivers and rivers swerved aside
And I grew desolate, and died.

At my hot breath they checked their rush
And reared a wave, a head, and hush . . .
Then fell and fled and would not come
To kiss the color of my loam.

The young bright rivers backed and fought —
And I lay thirsty and unsought.

They married valleys.   If I caught
Water in my hand, it seeped . . .
Rivers around — rain over me — leaped;
I was unwatered and unreaped.
Rather than take me for their bride
Rivers and rivers swerved aside
And I grew desolate, and died.

— (They shook their silver manes and curved
Aside.   Aside they swept and swerved
Past my dull grandeur.   River droves
Dared do no more than pound their hooves
And skirt my sombre purple. . . . White
Galloping cataracts took to flight.)

Why have I the lustre of stone?
Color of scorn, and scorn's tone
Brood over me.   I move beneath
Pale dust with an edged breath.

Sliding under cover of sand
I throttle young rivers with a bold hand.
Genevieve Taggard

HE WHO HAS KNOWN A RIVER

HE who has known a river in its dreaming,
Has watched it hushed with darkness, flushed with
     day;
Has seen the waves in molten moonlight streaming
Out to a quiet bay:

For whom, revealed beyond the river reaches,
Are islands whither sail was never blown,
Strange seas beyond the mist-enchanted beaches
Where gull has never flown:

Though he be banished, yet for him the river
Shall shine, for him shall sing and never cease;
Through all his thoughts there still shall flow forever
The moonlit waters of remembered peace.
Mary Sinton Leitch

JOHN BROWN

A NEGRO SERMON

I'VE been to Palestine.
   What did you see in Palestine?
I saw the ark of Noah —
It was made of pitch and pine.
I saw old Father Noah
Asleep beneath his vine.
I saw Shem, Ham and Japhet
Standing in a line.

I saw the tower of Babel
In the gorgeous sunrise shine —
By a weeping willow tree
Beside the Dead Sea.

I've been to Palestine.
What did you see in Palestine?
I saw abominations
And Gadarene swine.
I saw the sinful Canaanites
Upon the shewbread dine,
And spoil the temple vessels
And drink the temple wine.
I saw Lot's wife, a pillar of salt
Standing in the brine —
By a weeping willow tree
Beside the Dead Sea.

I've been to Palestine.
What did you see in Palestine?
Cedars on Mount Lebanon,
Gold in Ophir's mine,
And a wicked generation
Seeking for a sign
And Baal's howling worshippers
Their god with leaves entwine.
And . . .
I saw the war-horse ramping
And shake his forelock fine —
By a weeping willow tree
Beside the Dead Sea.

I've been to Palestine.
What did you see in Palestine?
Old John Brown.

Old John Brown.
I saw his gracious wife
Dressed in a homespun gown.
I saw his seven sons ˇ
Before his feet bow down.
And he marched with his seven sons,
His wagons and goods and guns,
To his campfire by the sea,
By the waves of Galilee.

I've been to Palestine.
    What did you see in Palestine?
I saw the harp and psalt'ry
Played for Old John Brown.
I heard the ram's horn blow,
Blow for Old John Brown.
I saw the Bulls of Bashan —
They cheered for Old John Brown.
I saw the big Behemoth —
He cheered for Old John Brown.
I saw the big Leviathan —
He cheered for Old John Brown.
I saw the Angel Gabriel
Great power to him assign.
I saw him fight the Canaanites
And set God's Israel free.
I saw him when the war was done
In his rustic chair recline —
By his campfire by the sea,
By the waves of Galilee.

I've been to Palestine.
    What did you see in Palestine?
Old John Brown.

Old John Brown.
And there he sits
To judge the world.
His hunting-dogs
At his feet are curled.
His eyes half-closed,
But John Brown sees
The ends of the earth,
The Day of Doom.
And his shot-gun lies
Across his knees —
Old John Brown,
Old John Brown.

Vachel Lindsay

HERITAGE

WHAT is Africa to me:
Copper sun or scarlet sea,
Jungle star or jungle track,
Strong bronzed men, or regal black
Women from whose loins I sprang
When the birds of Eden sang?
One three centuries removed
From the scenes his fathers loved,
Spicy grove, cinnamon tree,
What is Africa to me?

So I lie, who all day long
Want no sound except the song
Sung by wild barbaric birds
Goading massive jungle herds,
Juggernauts of flesh that pass
Trampling tall defiant grass

Where young forest lovers lie,
Plighting troth beneath the sky.
So I lie, who always hear,
Though I cram against my ear
Both my thumbs, and keep them there,
Great drums throbbing through the air.
So I lie, whose fount of pride,
Dear distress and joy allied,
Is my somber flesh and skin,
With the dark blood dammed within
Like great pulsing tides of wine
That, I fear, must burst the fine
Channels of the chafing net
Where they surge and foam and fret.

Africa? A book one thumbs
Listlessly, till slumber comes.
Unremembered are her bats
Circling through the night, her cats
Crouching in the river reeds,
Stalking gentle flesh that feeds
By the river brink; no more
Does the bugle-throated roar
Cry that monarch claws have leapt
From the scabbards where they slept.
Silver snakes that once a year
Doff the lovely coats you wear,
Seek no covert in your fear
Lest a mortal eye should see;
What's your nakedness to me?

Here no leprous flowers rear
Fierce corollas in the air;
Here no bodies sleek and wet,
Dripping mingled rain and sweat,

Tread the savage measures of
Jungle boys and girls in love.
What is last year's snow to me,
Last year's anything?   The tree
Budding yearly must forget
How its past arose or set —
Bough and blossom, flower, fruit,
Even what shy bird with mute
Wonder at her travail there,
Meekly labored in its hair.
One three centuries removed
From the scenes his fathers loved,
Spicy grove, cinnamon tree,
What is Africa to me?

So I lie, who find no peace
Night or day, no slight release
From the unremittent beat
Made by cruel padded feet
Walking through my body's street.
Up and down they go, and back,
Treading out a jungle track.
So I lie, who never quite
Safely sleep from rain at night —
I can never rest at all
When the rain begins to fall;
Like a soul gone mad with pain
I must match its weird refrain;
Ever must I twist and squirm,
Writhing like a baited worm,
While its primal measures drip
Through my body, crying, "Strip!
Doff this new exuberance.
Come and dance the Lover's Dance!"

In an old remembered way
Rain works on me night and day.

Quaint, outlandish heathen gods
Black men fashion out of rods,
Clay, and brittle bits of stone,
In a likeness like their own,
My conversion came high-priced;
I belong to Jesus Christ,
Preacher of humility;
Heathen gods are naught to me.

Father, Son, and Holy Ghost,
So I make an idle boast;
Jesus of the twice-turned cheek,
Lamb of God, although I speak
With my mouth thus, in my heart
Do I play a double part.
Ever at thy glowing altar
Must my heart grow sick and falter,
Wishing He I served were black,
Thinking then it would not lack
Precedent of pain to guide it,
Let who would or might deride it;
Surely then this flesh would know
Yours had borne a kindred woe.
Lord, I fashion dark gods, too,
Daring even to give You
Dark despairing features where,
Crowned with dark rebellious hair,
Patience wavers just so much as
Mortal grief compels, while touches
Quick and hot, of anger rise
To smitten cheek and weary eyes.

Lord, forgive me if my need
Sometimes shapes a human creed.

All day long and all night through,
One thing only must I do:
Quench my pride and cool my blood,
Lest I perish in the flood.
Lest a hidden ember set
Timber that I thought was wet
Burning like the dryest flax,
Melting like the merest wax,
Lest the grave restore its dead.
Not yet has my heart or head
In the least way realized
They and I are civilized.

Countee Cullen

CROSS

MY old man's a white old man
And my old mother's black.
If ever I cursed my white old man
I take my curses back.

If ever I cursed my black old mother
And wished she were in hell,
I'm sorry for that evil wish
And now I wish her well.

My old man died in a fine big house.
My ma died in a shack.
I wonder where I'm gonna die,
Being neither white nor black?

Langston Hughes

THE BIRD AND THE TREE

BLACKBIRD, blackbird in the cage,
There's something wrong tonight.
Far off the sheriff's footfall dies,
The minutes crawl like last year's flies
Between the bars, and like an age
The hours are long tonight.

The sky is like a heavy lid
Out here beyond the door tonight.
What's that? A mutter down the street.
What's that? A sound of yells and feet.
For what you didn't do or did
You'll pay the score tonight.

No use to wreak with reddened sweat,
No use to whimper and to sweat.
They've got the rope; they've got the guns,
They've got the courage and the guns;
And that's the reason why tonight;
No use to ask them any more.
They'll fire the answer through the door —
You're out to die tonight.

There where the lonely cross-road lies,
There is no place to make replies;
But silence, inch by inch, is there,
And the right limb for a lynch is there;
And a lean daw waits for both your eyes,
Blackbird.

Perhaps you'll meet again some place.
Look for the mask upon the face:
That's the way you'll know them there —
A white mask to hide the face.

And you can halt and show them there
The things that they are deaf to now,
And they can tell you what they meant —
To wash the blood with blood.   But how
If you are innocent?

Blackbird singer, blackbird mute,
They choked the seed you might have found.
Out of a thorny field you go —
For you it may be better so —
And leave the sowers of the ground
To eat the harvest of the fruit,
Blackbird.

Ridgely Torrence

THE EYES OF GOD

I SEE them nightly in my sleep.
The eyes of God are very deep.
There is no cave, no sea that knows
So much of unplumbed depth as those,
Or guards with walls or specters dumb
Such treasures for the venturesome.

I feel them burning on my back.
The eyes of God are very black.
There is no substance and no shade
So black as God his own eyes made;
In earth or heaven no night, no day
At once so black, so bright as they.

I see them wheresoe'er I turn.
The eyes of God are very stern.
The eyes of God are golden fires
That kindle beacons, kindle pyres;

And where like slow moon-rays they pass
They burn up dead things as dry grass.

They wait, and are not hard to find.
The eyes of God are very kind.
They have great pity for weak things
And joy in everything with wings;
And glow, beyond all telling bright,
Each time a brave soul dares a flight.

Hermann Hagedorn

DEATH RAY

THERE is that in the air, an imminence
Of things that hold the breath still and heart pale;
Naught that the mind affirms, but a fey sense
Illumines, and goes dark.   Can it avail
For men to follow what but dreams have had
In high and secret places — the dim torch
That Zarathustra blew on and went mad.
Was this the gleam that Jesus sought by night,
When he walked, veiled . . . in glamorous dim light
Washed, as a white goat before the slaughter. . . .
And heard no sound save the soft rhythmic beat
Upon the silken silence of his feet
Beautiful as gulls above the water.

Lola Ridge

SONNETS OF THE SAINTS

I

THE BLESSING OF COLUMCILLE

TORQUED warriors turned their galley's crimson prow
  To hear a white monk hymn the Holy Three
  In Derry's orchard vale beside the sea,

The light of peace upon his shining brow;
And angels, watching near the forest plough,
  Saw Colum's blessing change the withered tree,
  Cursed by the demon riders from the shee,
And bring the wild sweet apples to the bough.

Beneath his voice, clear as a ringing bell,
  Dark kerns laid down their spear-shafts, then were
    still,
    And in each bitter heart the sweet fruit grew;
Dim oak woods, wakened from the Druid spell,
  Shone white with wings; and on the sunset hill
    The old gods listened, lonely in the dew.

II

THE BRINDLED HARE

By grange and castle when the fields were cool
  Saint Anselm rode and marked how swans afloat
  Upon the lilied waters of the moat
Reposed in love untaught by rod or rule;
And while he paused beside the reedy pool,
  A brindled hare with blood upon her coat
  Took refuge from the pack's deep baying note
Beneath the scarlet housings of his mule.

But when the savage hunters sought their prey,
  At his command their hounds refused to spring,
    Held back like wolves within a forest snare;
And with bent bows, they watched him ride away,
  Tender as Christ Who heals each broken thing,
    Bearing against his breast the wounded hare.
                              Thomas S. Jones, Jr.

THE BUILDER

SMOOTHING a cypress beam
  With a scarred hand,
I saw a carpenter
  In a far land.

Down past the flat roofs
  Poured the white sun;
But still he bent his back,
  The patient one.

And I paused surprised
  In that queer place
To find an old man
  With a haunting face.

"Who art thou, carpenter,
  Of the bowed head;
And what buildest thou?"
  "Heaven," he said.

Willard Wattles

IN THE BEGINNING WAS THE WORD

IT took me ten days
To read the Bible through,
Then I saw what I saw,
And I knew what I knew.

I would rise before the dawn,
When the stars were in the sky;
I would go and read the Book,
Till the sun rode high.

In the silence of the noon,
I would read with a will.
I was one who had climbed
To an high, burning hill.

At dusk I fell asleep
With my head on the page.
Then I woke — then I read —
Till an hour seemed an age.

For a great wind blows
Through Ezekiel and John,
They are all one flesh
That the Spirit breathes upon.

And suddenly the words
Seemed to quicken and to shine;
They glowed like the bread,
They purpled like the wine.

Like bread that had been wheat
In a thousand ample plains,
Sown and harvested by men
From the suns — from the rains.

Like wine that had been grapes
In a thousand vineyards strong —
That was trampled by men's feet
With a shout, with a song.

Like the Bread, like the Wine,
That we eat with one accord —
The body and the blood
Of the supper of the Lord.

And the wine may be old
And the wine may be new —
But it all is the Lord's —
And I knew what I knew.

For a great wind blows
Through Ezekiel and John,
They are all one flesh
That the Spirit breathes upon.

And a letter is a power,
And a name is a rune —
And an alphabet, my friends,
Is a strange and ancient tune.

And each letter is a throne
From which fearful splendors stream —
I could see them flash like fire
With an arch-angelic gleam.

And within each word a city
Shone more far than eye could reach —
Where the people glowed like stars
With a great new speech.

And each city was an angel,
And they sang with one accord —
Crying, "Holy, holy, holy,"
In the presence of the Lord.

The Book felt like flesh,
It would breathe — it would sing —
It would throb beneath my hand
Like a bird, like a wing.

It would cry, it would groan,
It would shout and complain, —
It would seem to climb a hill
With its solemn stress of pain.

It would grapple with fierce powers,
With a deep interior strife.
It would seem to heave and lift
With a terrible, glad life.

And my flesh was in the Book,
And its blood was in me;
I could feel it throb within,
As plain as it could be.

I was filled with its powers,
And I cried all alone,
"The Lord is in the tomb,
And my body is the stone."

I was anguished, I was dumb,
When the powers began to move,
That shall stir the aching ground,
That shall shake the earth with love.

Then my flesh, which was the stone,
Felt the hills begin to lift.
The seas shook and heaved,
And the stars began to shift.

And the words rushed on
And each letter was a throne.
They swept through my flesh,
Through my brain, through my bone,

With a great, fearful rush,
I felt it clean through.

Oh, I saw what I saw,
And I knew what I knew.

And I swung one side
When the ghostly power began.
Then the Book stood up —
And I saw it was a Man.

For a great wind blows
Through Ezekiel and John.
They are all one flesh
That the Spirit breathes upon.
It took me ten days
To read the Bible through —
Then I saw what I saw,
And I knew what I knew.

Anna Hempstead Branch

A PAGAN REINVOKES THE TWENTY–THIRD PSALM

I KNOCK again and try again the key,
I, who, enraged, fled from Thy temple's trees
Because the presence of my enemies
Around the table there offended me.
I, who laid up so long and bitterly
Complaints and old reproaches, on my knees
Offer regret for years misspent as these,
And wonder how such folly came to be.
Anoint again my head and let me walk
The valley of the shadow, with the rod
Thou hast afforded for my comfort, God:
My soul restored, and singing through my veins.
Forgive the years of idle, foolish talk:
The cup that runneth over still remains.

Robert Wolf

LAST SUPPER: JESUS TO JUDAS

In no one sin couldst thou abide,
Door after door thou still hast tried;
Nor will the gold of avarice
Unlock the earthly Paradise.

And yet rejoice: this is the last
And deepest sin that must be passed;
For till man bitterly has priced
In Caesar's coin the living Christ,
He cannot kill himself for me
And with his corpse buy Charity.
That price unpaid, he still must dwell
Within the hidden flames of Hell,
And I shall see I came in vain,
So sacrifice myself again.

I knew, when wine from water ran,
That I must die, for man is man;
I knew, when wine was changed to blood,
That I must die, for I am God.
I chose thee, and I chose thee well,
To do this deed; since thou wilt sell
For hate the thing that thou wilt buy

Again for love most bitterly.
Then shalt thou kill thyself for me,
And greater love there cannot be.
And now thy Passion must begin.
Fear not: let Satan enter in.
(Long since have I forgiven thee;
But how soon wilt thou pardon me?)

I gave the purse, that it might brim
With silver of the Sanhedrim.
I washed thy feet, for I shall feel
The weight of the triumphant heel.
O silent one, take what is thine
— This last sop of the bread and wine —
To bless the deed; because a Tree
Is now prepared also for thee.

                              S. Foster Damon

THE WIFE OF JUDAS ISCARIOT

THE wife of Judas Iscariot
    Went out into the night,
She thought she heard a voice crying:
    Was it to left or right?

She went forth to the Joppa Gate,
    Three crosses hung on high.
The one was a thief's, the other a thief's,
    The third she went not nigh.

For still she heard the voice crying:
    Was it to right or left?
Or was it but a wind of fear
    That blew her on bereft?

She went down from the Joppa Gate
    Into the black ravine.
She climbed up by the rocky path
    To where a tree was seen.

And 'What, sooth, do I follow here?
    Is it my own mad mind?
Judas!   Judas Iscariot!'
    She called upon the wind.

'Judas! Judas Iscariot!'
　　She crept beneath the tree.
What thing was it that swung there,
　　Hung so dolorously?

'Judas! Judas Iscariot!'
　　She touched it with her hand.
The leaves shivered above her head
　　To make her understand.

'Judas! Judas! my love! my lord!'
　　Her hands went o'er it fast,
From foot to thigh, from thigh to throat,
　　And stopped — there — at last.

'Judas! Judas! what has He done,
　　The Christ you followed so!'
More than the silver left on him
　　Made answer to her woe.

'Judas! Judas! what has He done!
　　O has it come to this!
The Kingdom promised has but proved
　　For you a soul-abyss!

'Was He the Christ and let it be?' . . .
　　She cut him from the limb,
And held him in her arms there
　　And wept over him,

'None in the world shall ever know
　　Your doubts of Him but I!
"Traitor! traitor! and only traitor!"
　　Will ever be their cry!

'None in the world shall ever know —
  But I who am your wife!'
She flung the silver from his purse:
  It made a bitter strife.

It rattled on the ringing rocks
  And fell to the ravine.
'Was He the Christ and let it be?'
  She moaned, still, between.

She held him in her arms there,
  And kissed his lips aright,
The lips of Judas Iscariot,
  Who hanged himself that night.

Cale Young Rice

OUR THIRTY PIECES

A CHANT of dark betrayals: song betrayed
By those who turned their backs against its morn;
Of art conceived, yet left at birth forlorn
By hearts that feared the thing their dreams had made,
Of an unsanctioned parentage afraid;
Of music silenced by the world's dumb scorn;
Of banners up the light no longer borne
Lest mock of fools might darken the parade.

And yet who dares to chide them — these, who failed,
Reluctant, at the opening verge of bliss,
Because the censures of the world prevailed?
For who has not betrayed enough to know
How Judas drank immeasurable woe
Of broken love, with one most hapless kiss?

Harry Kemp

I HEARD IMMANUEL SINGING

I HEARD Immanuel singing
Within his own good lands,
I saw him bend above his harp,
I watched his wandering hands
Lost amid the harp-strings;
Sweet, sweet I heard him play.
His wounds were altogether healed.
Old things had passed away.

All things were new, but music.
The blood of David ran
Within the son of David,
Our God, the Son of Man.
He was ruddy like a shepherd.
His bold young face, how fair.
Apollo of the silver bow
Had not such flowing hair.

I saw Immanuel singing
On a tree-girdled hill.
The glad remembering branches
Dimly echoed still
The grand new song proclaiming
The Lamb that had been slain.
New-built, the Holy City
Gleamed in the murmuring plain.

The crowning hours were over.
The pageants all were past.
Within the many mansions
The hosts, grown still at last,
In homes of holy mystery

Slept long by crooning springs
Or waked to peaceful glory,
A universe of Kings.

He left his people happy.
He wandered free to sigh
Alone in lowly friendship
With the green grass and the sky.
He murmured ancient music
His red heart burned to sing
Because his perfect conquest
Had grown a weary thing.

No chant of gilded triumph —
His lonely song was made
Of Art's deliberate freedom;
Of minor chords arrayed
In soft and shadowy colors
That once were radiant flowers: —
The Rose of Sharon, bleeding,
In Olive-shadowed bowers: —

And all the other roses
In the songs of East and West
Of love and war and worshipping,
And every shield and crest
Of thistle or of lotus
Or sacred lily wrought
In creeds and psalms and palaces
And temples of white thought: —

All these he sang, half-smiling
And weeping as he smiled,
Laughing, talking to his harp
As to a new-born child: —

As though the arts forgotten
But bloomed to prophesy
These careless, fearless harp-strings,
New-crying in the sky.
"When this his hour of sorrow
For flowers and Arts of men
Has passed in ghostly music,"
I asked my wild heart then —

What will he sing tomorrow,
What wonder all his own,
Alone, set free, rejoicing,
With a green hill for his throne?
What will he sing tomorrow,
What wonder all his own,
Alone, set free, rejoicing,
With a green hill for his throne?

Vachel Lindsay

ONE VERSION

I THINK that Mary Magdalene
Was just a woman who went to dine,
And her jewels covered her empty heart
And her gown was the color of wine.

I think that Mary Magdalene
Sat by a stranger with shining head.
"Haven't we met somewhere?" she asked.
Magdalene! — Mary! he said.

I think that Mary Magdalene
Fell at his feet and called his name,
Sat at his feet and wept her woe
And rose up clean of shame.

Nobody knew but Magdalene,
Mary the woman who went to dine,
Nobody saw how he broke the bread
And poured for her peace the wine.

This is the story of Magdalene;
It's not the tale the Apostles tell,
But I know the woman it happened to —
I know the woman well.

Leonora Speyer

LOST HARBOR

For George Sterling

THE love of life that captained him could brook
No laggard helm aversive to the gale;
He knew the fleetness of the wind, the look
Of decks aslant under a cloud of sail.
So, when the sea came sucking at the seams,
And mutiny like some dark plague began
Muttering through the turmoil of his dreams,
He sought a harbor where the slow tides ran.

There is a port of no return, where ships
May ride at anchor for a little space.
And then, some starless night, the cable slips,
Leaving an eddy at the mooring place . . .
Gulls, veer no longer. Sailor, rest your oar.
No tangled wreckage will be washed ashore.

Leslie Nelson Jennings

SAUL

WEEP for the one so strong to slay, whom One has
    taken at last!
Mourn for the mail that rings no more and the ruin
    unforecast!
This was he of the flaming heart and the deep, heroic
    breath,
Whose sword is laid and his armor hung in the House
    of Ashtoreth.

Weep for the one so swift to slay, whose knees have
    bent to the night!
Dust is thick on his thresholds now, though trumpets
    call to the fight.
Slinger and bowman gather fast, but our strong man
    does not come.
Captains long for his counsels now, but the sated lips
    are dumb.

Cry his name in the citadel, sending the runners forth:
The South gives back no rumor of him; in vain they
    question the North.
Seek him not where the wall is held or the spears go in
    to death,
Whose shield is laid and his armor hung in the House
    of Ashtoreth.

This was he grown mighty in war, but her war is
    otherwise:
Swords that flash from her bosom bared, arrows cast
    from her eyes.
Who shall stoop from her javelin thrown, who from
    her singing dart?
Her sudden shaft is hot in his loins, her steel in his
    maddened heart.

Deep in the still and altared dusk her lamp glows
  small and red,
Mirrored clear in the great cuirass, like the rubies of
  her bed;
Blood of light on his burnished helm, on the belt and
  the greaves, one saith,
Whose spear is laid and his armor hung in the House
  of Ashtoreth.

Though Gath go up to the threshing-floors, or hosts
  assemble at Tyre,
Wait no more for your prince's word, who has taken
  his desire.
Cities and fields and given hearts, honor and life
  were weighed,
The balance shown and the end foreseen and the deep
  decision made.

Weep for the one so strong in war, whose war is now
  of the Dark!
Well he harnessed his breast with steel, but her arrows
  find their mark.
Her hands have loosened the brazen belt and her
  breath has found his breath
Whose sword is laid and his armor hung in the House
  of Ashtoreth.

George Sterling

DAVID

I HAVE been drunk of life's commingled wines,
Of lilied loves and rose-red concubines.
I have known battle and the white-hot charm
Of holding death at bay with this right arm.
I have known pomp and purpled pride and cries
Of clamorous applause against the skies.

I have been overwrought and overjoyed,
I have been sated, surfeited, and cloyed.
In my own life I've lived so many lives
Its flames are cinders, yet one spark survives.
Gold, glory, greed! I loved you not for long;
Wine, women, war! seductive, but not strong;
One passion lasts — the deathless lust of Song.
Edmund Vance Cooke

THAT HARP YOU PLAY SO WELL

O DAVID, if I had
Your power, I should be glad —
    In harping, with the sling,
    In patient reasoning!

Blake, Homer, Job, and you,
Have made old wine-skins new.
    Your energies have wrought
    Stout continents of thought.

But, David, if the heart
Be brass, what boots the art
    Of exorcising wrong,
    Of harping to a song?

The sceptre and the ring
And every royal thing
    Will fail.   Grief's lustiness
    Must cure the harp's distress.
Marianne Moore

HEBREWS

I COME of a mighty race. . . . I come of a very mighty
    race. . . .
Adam was a mighty man, and Noah a captain of the
    moving waters,
Moses was a stern and splendid king, yea, so was
    Moses.
Give me more songs like David's to shake my throat
    to the pit of the belly,
And let me roll in the Isaiah thunder. . . .

Ho! the mightiest of our young men was born under
    a star in the midwinter. . . .
His name is written on the sun and it is frosted on
    the moon. . . .
Earth breathes him like an eternal spring: he is a
    second sky over the Earth.

Mighty race! mighty race! — my flesh, my flesh
Is a cup of song,
Is a well in Asia. . . .
I go about with a dark heart where the Ages sit in
    a divine thunder. . . .
My blood is cymbal-clashed and the anklets of the
    dancers tinkle there. . . .
Harp and psaltery, harp and psaltery make drunk
    my spirit. . . .

I am of the terrible people, I am of the strange
    Hebrews. . . .
Amongst the swarms fixed like the rooted stars, my
    folk is a streaming Comet,
Comet of the Asian tiger-darkness,
The Wanderer of Eternity, the eternal Wandering
    Jew. . . .

Ho! we have turned against the mightiest of our
    young men
And in that denial we have taken on the Christ,
And the two thieves beside the Christ,
And the Magdalen at the feet of the Christ,
And the Judas with thirty silver pieces selling the
    Christ, —
And our twenty centuries in Europe have the shape
    of a Cross
On which we have hung in disaster and glory. . . .

Mighty race! mighty race! my flesh, my flesh
Is a cup of song,
Is a well in Asia.

                              James Oppenheim

BOUGH OF BABYLON

How shall I sing whose harp-strings rot upon
The old habitual bough of Babylon —
The exile's branch where no tears can appease
The inarticulate and iron trees?
Malignant beauty locked in the cold bough
Never so cold as now.

How shall I sing in a strange land, alone
With time like water dribbling over stone,
And in my heart a small recurrent sound
Like water eating stubborn edges round?
To some grief brings a trumpet's throat, to some —
"O my son Absalom!

O Abalsom my son!"   O harp as dead!
O flutes forever choking in my head!

Where is that laughter? Shall I hear again
The dark sonorous music of that brain? . . .
The bough of Babylon is dripping cold;
This heart is old.

Joseph Auslander

CASTILIAN

VELASQUEZ took a pliant knife
And scraped his palette clean;
Said he, "I lead a dog's own life
Painting a king and queen."

He cleaned his palette with oily rags
And oakum from Seville wharves;
"I am sick of painting painted hags
And bad ambiguous dwarves.

"The sky is silver, the clouds are pearl,
Their locks are looped with rain.
I will not paint Maria's girl
For all the money in Spain."

He washed his face in water cold,
His hands in turpentine;
He squeezed out color like coins of gold
And color like drops of wine.

Each color lay like a little pool
On the polished cedar wood;
Clear and pale and ivory-cool
Or dark as solitude.

He burnt the rags in the fireplace
And leaned from the window high;
He said, "I like that gentleman's face
Who wears his cap awry."

This is the gentleman, there he stands,
Castilian, sombre-caped,
With arrogant eyes, and narrow hands
Miraculously shaped.

Elinor Wylie

ZULOAGA

SARDONIC master, you that dare betray
  With piercing vision and relentless hand
  The mournful features of a sombre land
Where youth and love and hope have had their day;
Your silken senoritas, lissome, gay,
  With soulless eyes inanimately bland;
  Your tinsel toreadors that idly stand
Against the mountain's monotone of gray; —

What are they but the puppets of romance
  Worn threadbare, tarnished by an evil time;
But gallant still for all their sad mischance,
A pageant of the glories that remain
  Where towered once, exultant and sublime,
The grim and splendid chivalry of Spain.

Charles Wharton Stork

MR. POPE

WHEN Alexander Pope strolled in the city
Strict was the glint of pearl and gold sedans.
Ladies leaned out, more out of fear than pity;
For Pope's tight back was rather a goat's than man's.

Often one thinks the urn should have more bones
Than skeletons provide for speedy dust;
The urn gets hollow, cobwebs brittle as stones
Weave to the funeral shell a frivolous rust.

And he who dribbled couplets like a snake
Coiled to a lithe precision in the sun,
Is missing.   The jar is empty; you may break
It only to find that Mr. Pope is gone.

What requisitions of a verity
Prompted the wit and rage between his teeth
One cannot say.   Around a crooked tree
A moral climbs whose name should be a wreath.

Allen Tate

PORCELAINE DE SAXE

Petite Madame, your smiling face
Serenely scorns the commonplace,
And you, Monsieur, your bow is quite
The fine quintessence of polite!

In seventeen seventy you showed
Your garments as the latest mode, —
Panniers and puffs and fine plumed hat,
Buckles and bows and lace cravat —

But he who made you never guessed
That Time, who loves a sorry jest,
Destroying kings and monarchies,
Would spare you, gay futilities.

How many a timely circumstance
Has saved you from the swift mischance
Which would have left your pieces scattered,
And all your china graces shattered!

The busy housewife, in a fluster, —
A maid's far flung, impetuous duster, —
Twixt you and these still intervenes
The god of foolish figurines.

I shrug, but ruefully.   Alas!
When I, and all of mine, shall pass,
Still in the best ceramic style
Monsieur shall bow, Madame shall smile!
                              Virginia Lyne Tunstall

FOR ANY LADY'S BIRTHDAY

SPRING's silver poplars stand apart,
Most ladylike of trees,
And mortal ladies should take heart
From gentlefolk like these.

They watch the blue days pass along,
They see the nights go by,
But keep forever morning's song
And nighttime's starry sky.

They know the maiden spring goes soon,
But their wise hearts are still,
For they have seen the quiet moon
Above a wooded hill.

The poplars wear in halo-guise
Their silver crown of years —
And if all ladies were as wise
There would be fewer tears.
                              Lawrence Lee

PIAZZA PIECE

— I AM a gentleman in a dustcoat trying
To make you hear.   Your ears are soft and small
And listen to an old man not at all,
They want the young men's whispering and sighing.

But see the roses on your trellis dying
And hear the spectral singing of the moon;
For I must have my lovely lady soon.
I am a gentleman in a dustcoat trying.

— I am a lady young in beauty waiting
Until my truelove comes, and then we kiss.
But what grey man among the vines is this
Whose words are dry and faint as in a dream?
Back from my trellis, sir, before I scream!
I am a lady young in beauty waiting.

John Crowe Ransom

FOR ALL LADIES OF SHALOTT

THE web flew out and floated wide.
   Poor lady! I was with her then.
She gathered up her piteous pride,
   But she could never weave again.

The mirror cracked from side to side;
   I saw its silver shadows go.
"The curse has come on me!" she cried.
   Poor lady! I had told her so.

She was so proud: she would not hide.
   She only laughed and tried to sing.
But singing, in her song she died.
   She did not profit anything.

Aline Kilmer

PORTRAIT OF A LADY

Thou hast committed
Fornication: but that was in another country,
And besides, the wench is dead.

THE JEW OF MALTA

I

Among the smoke and fog of a December afternoon
You have the scene arrange itself — as it will seem
　　to do —
With "I have saved this afternoon for you";
And four wax candles in the darkened room,
Four rings of light upon the ceiling overhead,
An atmosphere of Juliet's tomb
Prepared for all the things to be said, or left unsaid.
We have been, let us say, to hear the latest Pole
Transmit the Preludes, through his hair and
　　　　finger-tips.
"So intimate, this Chopin, that I think his soul
Should be resurrected only among friends
Some two or three, who will not touch the bloom
That is rubbed and questioned in the concert room."
— And so the conversation slips
Among velleities and carefully caught regrets
Through attenuated tones of violins
Mingled with remote cornets
And begins.

"You do not know how much they mean to me, my
　　　　friends,
And how, how rare and strange it is, to find
In a life composed so much, so much of odds and ends,
(For indeed I do not love it . . . you knew? you are
　　　　not blind!　How keen you are!)
To find a friend who has these qualities,
Who has, and gives
Those qualities upon which friendship lives.
How much it means that I say this to you —
Without these friendships — life, what *cauche-mar!*"

Among the windings of the violins
And the ariettes
Of cracked cornets
Inside my brain a dull tom-tom begins
Absurdly hammering a prelude of its own,
Capricious monotone
That is at least one definite "false note."
Let us take the air, in a tobacco trance,
Admire the monuments
Discuss the late events,
Correct our watches by the public clocks.
Then sit for half an hour and drink our bocks.

II

Now that lilacs are in bloom
She has a bowl of lilacs in her room
And twists one in her fingers while she talks.
"Ah, my friend, you do not know, you do not know
What life is, you should hold it in your hands";
(Slowly twisting the lilac stalks)
"You let it flow from you, you let it flow,
And youth is cruel, and has no remorse
And smiles at situations which it cannot see."
I smile, of course,
And go on drinking tea.
"Yet with these April sunsets, that somehow recall
My buried life, and Paris in the Spring,
I feel immeasurably at peace, and find the world
To be wonderful and youthful, after all."

The voice returns like the insistent out-of-tune
Of a broken violin on an August afternoon:
"I am always sure that you understand

My feelings, always sure that you feel,
Sure that across the gulf you reach your hand.

You are invulnerable, you have no Achilles' heel.
You will go on, and when you have prevailed
You can say: at this point many a one has failed.

But what have I, but what have I, my friend,
To give you, what can you receive from me?
Only the friendship and the sympathy
Of one about to reach her journey's end.

I shall sit here, serving tea to friends. . . ."
I take my hat: how can I make a cowardly amends
For what she has said to me?
You will see me any morning in the park
Reading the comics and the sporting page.
Particularly I remark
An English countess goes upon the stage.
A Greek was murdered at a Polish dance,
Another bank defaulter has confessed.
I keep my countenance,
I remain self-possessed
Except when a street piano, mechanical and tired
Reiterates some worn-out common song
With the smell of hyacinths across the garden
Recalling things that other people have desired.
Are these ideas right or wrong?

III

The October night comes down; returning as before
Except for a slight sensation of being ill at ease
I mount the stairs and turn the handle of my door
And feel as if I had mounted on my hands and knees.

"And so you are going abroad; and when do you
     return?
But that's a useless question.
You hardly know when you are coming back,
You will find so much to learn."
My smile falls heavily among the bric-à-brac.

"Perhaps you can write to me."
My self-possession flares up for a second;
This is as I had reckoned.
"I have been wondering frequently of late
(But our beginnings never know our ends!)
Why we have not developed into friends."
I feel like one who smiles, and turning shall remark
Suddenly, his expression in a glass.
My self-possession gutters; we are really in the dark.

"For everybody said so, all our friends,
They all were sure our feelings would relate
So closely! I myself can hardly understand.
We must leave it now to fate.
You will write, at any rate.
Perhaps it is not too late.
I shall sit here, serving tea to friends."

And I must borrow every changing shape
To find expression . . . dance, dance
Like a dancing bear,
Cry like a parrot, chatter like an ape.
Let us take the air, in a tobacco trance —
Well! and what if she should die some afternoon,
Afternoon grey and smoky, evening yellow and rose;
Should die and leave me sitting pen in hand
With the smoke coming down above the house-tops;

Doubtful, for quite a while
Not knowing what to feel or if I understand
Or whether wise or foolish, tardy or too soon . . .
Would she not have the advantage, after all?
This music is successful with a "dying fall"
Now that we talk of dying —
And should I have the right to smile?

T. S. Eliot

JOAN OF ARC, 1926

I HAVE no solid horse to share with Joan,
I have no wit to contradict a duke
If there were dukes; I dream my dreams alone,
And cannot, in the face of Rome's rebuke,
Consider them divine.   Rather I know
That nations are not worth the men they break,
And tardy Joans are destined to forego
Danger, and the incentive of the stake.

But I shall ride — most surely I shall ride —
Across a field more difficult than France,
Sternly, upon a horse that is my pride,
And make a sword of each foul circumstance
To conquer half the world disdainfully
Before a world, prescribed, can conquer me!

Virginia Moore

DEFIANCE TO FALSE GODS

You do not like my altar smoke,
Nor find me bent enough in prayer;
Is it for this that you invoke
Sorrow to bend me with despair?

No gaudy tribute do I pay,
Nor hurt my voice to sing your praise;
Is it for this that you display
Pain that can quench my burning days?

Or is it that I dared to ask
Why I was made, and to what end
You gave short days for my long task,
When you'd eternity to lend?

So will I question, nor be done
Till I fall weary, and submit —
I, who was once oblivion,
And straightway must return to it!

Bernice Lesbia Kenyon

SONGS

ALWAYS before your voice my soul
half-beautiful and wholly droll
is as some smooth and awkward foal,
whereof young moons begin
the newness of his skin,

so of my stupid sincere youth
the exquisite failure uncouth
discovers a trembling and smooth
Unstrength, against the strong
silences of your song;

or as a single lamb whose sheen
of full unsheared fleece is mean
beside its lovelier friends, between
your thoughts more white than wool
My thought is sorrowful:

but my heart smote in trembling thirds
of anguish quivers to your words,
As to a flight of thirty birds
shakes with a thickening fright
the sudden fooled light.

it is the autumn of a year:
When through the thin air stooped with fear,
across the harvest whitely peer
empty of surprise
death's faultless eyes

(whose hand my folded soul shall know
while on faint hills do frailly go
The peaceful terrors of the snow,
and before your dead face
which sleeps, a dream shall pass)

and these my days their sounds and flowers
Fall in a pride of petaled hours,
like flowers at the feet of mowers
whose bodies strong with love
through meadows hugely move.

yet what am i that such and such
mysteries very simply touch
me, whose heart-wholeness overmuch
Expects of your hair pale,
a terror musical?

while in an earthless hour my fond
soul seriously yearns beyond
this fern of sunset frond on frond
opening in a rare
Slowness of gloried air . . .

The flute of morning stilled in noon —
noon the implacable bassoon —
now Twilight seeks the thrill of moon,
washed with a wild and thin
despair of violin.

                                        E. E. Cummings

AS HELEN ONCE

THE east unrolled a sheet of gold,
    Gold for river and flower and limb;
As Helen once to Paris was
    Was I to him.

All things gold fade gray and old,
    Even the sun of love grows dim;
As Helen now to Paris is
    Am I to him.

                                        Muna Lee

INTERVALS

I SHALL make offering in a new basket of marsh-grass
Curved like a conch-shell, sharp with salt echoes,
Two long handles like looped arms.
Untamed things shall I bring to the god of gardens,
Plum-blossom, sweet-olive and thyme,
Tang of small figs, gone wild in deserted gardens,
Most subtle of trees as the serpent is subtlest of beasts,
Slouched on the heat-soaked walls . . .
I shall lay them under the weary, appraising eyes,
The cynical musical fingers
That rest on the goat-thighs.
Let me give him, O Pan,
All in the way of love —

The new keen edge of difference,
The wonder of being together,
And the wild taste of immemorial marsh-grass.
But in the intervals,
When the lover is gone and only the comrade remains,
Pan, have mercy!
Teach me to talk like a man!

Beatrice Ravenel

DREAM

You should have weighted my dream of you
With a leaden reality,
Then it would have gone down
Like some shotted mariner
Stark in his canvas,
Leaving the following seas
All open to the stars!

Being only a dream,
There's never a wave
Lifting from blue to chrysoprase,
Never an opal shine on the wet beaches,
Nor auklet shattering
The twilight's pure obsidian,
Never a swift wing flash of beauty anywhere
But my dream of you is there.

Mary Austin

MEN LOVED WHOLLY BEYOND WISDOM

MEN loved wholly beyond wisdom
Have the staff without the banner.
Like a fire in a dry thicket
Rising within women's eyes

Is the love men must return.
Heart, so subtle now, and trembling,
What a marvel to be wise,
To love never in this manner!
To be quiet in the fern
Like a thing gone dead and still,
Listening to the prisoned cricket
Shake its terrible, dissembling
Music in the granite hill.

Louise Bogan

SONNET TO A PLOW–WOMAN OF NORWAY

DEEP-BOSOMED, stalwart-limbed, superbly made,
Unconscious of her power and her grace,
Accustomed to the blowzy wind's embrace,
Magnificent, unlettered, unafraid.
She guides her course past interlacing streams
Striding the fields behind her ancient plow,
Or halts beneath some blossoming, frail bough
To rest her beast and give herself to dreams.
Her eyes survey the road, the moor, the peat,
With wide, untroubled gaze; she plays no part,
No joys rise up to suffocate her heart
Because a smile falls lightly at her feet.
To one who comes for her at dusk, perchance,
She lifts a brief, intoxicated glance.

Margaret Tod Ritter

THE MOUNTAIN WOMAN

AMONG the sullen peaks she stood at bay
And paid life's hard account from her small store.
Knowing the code of mountain wives, she bore
The burden of the days without a sigh;

And, sharp against the somber winter sky,
I saw her drive her steers afield each day.

Hers was the hand that sunk the furrows deep
Across the rocky, grudging southern slope.
At first youth left her face, and later, hope;
Yet through each mocking spring and barren fall,
She reared her lusty brood, and gave them all
That gladder wives and mothers love to keep.

And when the sheriff shot her eldest son
Beside his still, so well she knew her part,
She gave no healing tears to ease her heart;
But took the blow upstanding, with her eyes
As drear and bitter as the winter skies.
Seeing her then, I thought that she had won.

But yesterday her man returned too soon
And found her tending, with a reverent touch,
One scarlet bloom; and, having drunk too much,
He snatched its flame and quenched it in the dirt.
Then, like a creature with a mortal hurt,
She fell, and wept away the afternoon.

Du Bose Heyward

THE MOUNTAIN WHIPPOORWILL

UP in the mountains, it's lonesome all the time,
(Sof' win' slewin' thu' the sweet-potato vine.)

Up in the mountains, it's lonesome for a child,
(Whippoorwills a-callin' when the sap runs wild.)

Up in the mountains, mountains in the fog,
Everythin's as lazy as an old houn' dog.

Born in the mountains, never raised a pet,
Don't want nuthin' an' never got it yet.

Born in the mountains, lonesome-born,
Raised runnin' ragged thu' the cockleburrs and corn.

Never knew my pappy, mebbe never should.
Think he was a fiddle made of mountain laurel-wood.

Never had a mammy to teach me pretty-please.
Think she was a whippoorwill, a-skitin' thu' the trees.

Never had a brother ner a whole pair of pants,
But when I start to fiddle, why, yuh got to start to
     dance!

Listen to my fiddle — Kingdom Come — Kingdom
    Come!
Hear the frogs a-chunkin' "Jug o' rum, Jug o' rum!"
Hear that mountain-whippoorwill be lonesome in the air,
An' I'll tell yuh how I travelled to the Essex County Fair.

Essex County has a mighty pretty fair,
All the smarty fiddlers from the South come there.

Elbows flyin' as they rosin up the bow
For the First Prize Contest in the Georgia Fiddlers'
     Show.

Old Dan Wheeling with his whiskers in his ears,
King-pin fiddler for nearly twenty years.

Big Tom Sargent, with his blue wall-eye,
An' Little Jimmy Weezer that can make a fiddle cry.

All sittin' roun', spittin' high an' struttin' proud,
(Listen, little whippoorwill, yuh better bug yore eyes!)
Tun-a-tun-a-tunin' while the jedges told the crowd
Them that got the mostest claps'd win the bestest prize.

Everybody waitin' for the first tweedle-dee,
When in comes a-stumblin' — hill-billy me!

Bowed right pretty to the jedges an' the rest,
Took a silver dollar from a hole inside my vest,

Plunked it on the table an' said, "There's my callin'
    card!"
An' anyone that licks me — well, he's got to fiddle
    hard!

Old Dan Wheeling, he was laughin' fit to holler,
Little Jimmy Weezer said, "There's one dead dollar!"

Big Tom Sargent had a yaller-toothy grin,
But I tucked my little whippoorwill spang underneath
    my chin,
An' petted it an' tuned it till the jedges said, "Begin!"

Big Tom Sargent was the first in line;
He could fiddle all the bugs off a sweet-potato-vine.

He could fiddle down a possum from a mile-high tree.
He could fiddle up a whale from the bottom of the sea.

Yuh could hear hands spankin' till they spanked each
    other raw,
When he finished variations on "Turkey in the Straw."

Little Jimmy Weezer was the next to play;
He could fiddle all night, he could fiddle all day.

He could fiddle chills, he could fiddle fever,
He could make a fiddle rustle like a lowland river.

He could make a fiddle croon like a lovin' woman.
An' they clapped like thunder when he'd finished
    strummin'.

Then came the ruck of the bob-tailed fiddlers,
The let's-go-easies, the fair-to-middlers.

They got their claps an' they lost their bicker,
An' settled back for some more corn-licker.

An' the crowd was tired of their no-count squealing,
When out in the center steps Old Dan Wheeling.

He fiddled high and he fiddled low,
(Listen, little whippoorwill, yuh got to spread yore
    wings!)
He fiddled with a cherrywood bow.
(Old Dan Wheeling's got bee-honey in his strings.)

He fiddled the wind by the lonesome moon,
He fiddled a most almighty tune.

He started fiddling like a ghost,
He ended fiddling like a host.

He fiddled north an' he fiddled south,
He fiddled the heart right out of yore mouth.

He fiddled here an' he fiddled there.
He fiddled salvation everywhere.

When he was finished, the crowd cut loose,
(Whippoorwill, they's rain on yore breast.)
An' I sat there wonderin' "What's the use?"
(Whippoorwill, fly home to yore nest.)

But I stood up pert an' I took my bow,
An' my fiddle went to my shoulder, so.

An' — they wasn't no crowd to get me fazed —
But I was alone where I was raised.

Up in the mountains, so still it makes yuh skeered,
Where God lies sleepin' in his big white beard.

An' I heard the sound of the squirrel in the pine,
An' I heard the earth a-breathin' thu' the long night-
time.

They've fiddled the rose, an' they've fiddled the thorn,
But they haven't fiddled the mountain-corn.

They've fiddled sinful an' fiddled moral,
But they haven't fiddled the breshwood-laurel.

They've fiddled loud, and they've fiddled still,
But they haven't fiddled the whippoorwill.

I started off with a *dump-diddle-dump*,
(*Oh, hell's broke loose in Georgia!*)
Skunk-cabbage growin' by the bee-gum stump,
(*Whippoorwill, yo're singin' now!*)
Oh, Georgia booze is mighty fine booze,
The best yuh ever poured yuh,
But it eats the soles right offen yore shoes,
For hell's broke loose in Georgia.
My mother was a whippoorwill pert,
My father, he was lazy,
But I'm hell broke loose in a new store shirt
To fiddle all Georgia crazy.

Swing yore partners — up an' down the middle!
Sashay now — oh, listen to that fiddle!
Flapjacks flippin' on a red-hot griddle,
An' hell broke loose,
Hell broke loose,
Fire on the mountains — snakes in the grass,

Satan's here a-bilin' — oh, Lordy, let him pass!
Go down Moses, set my people free,
Pop goes the weasel thu' the old Red Sea!
Jonah sittin' on a hickory-bough,
Up jumps a whale — an' where's yore prophet now?
Rabbit in the pea-patch, possum in the pot,
Try an' stop my fiddle, now my fiddle's gettin' hot!
Whippoorwill, singin' thu' the mountain hush,
Whippoorwill, shoutin' from the burnin' bush,
Whippoorwill, cryin' in the stable-door,
Sing tonight as yuh never sang before!
Hell's broke loose like a stompin' mountain-shoat,
Sing till yuh bust the gold in yore throat!
Hell's broke loose for forty miles aroun'
Bound to stop yore music if yuh don't sing it down.
Sing on the mountains, little whippoorwill,
Sing to the valleys, an' slap 'em with a hill,
For I'm struttin' high as an eagle's quill,
An' hell's broke loose,
Hell's broke loose,
Hell's broke loose in Georgia!

They wasn't a sound when I stopped bowin',
(*Whippoorwill, yuh can sing no more.*)
But, somewhere or other, the dawn was growin'.
(*Oh, mountain whippoorwill!*)

An' I thought, "I've fiddled all night an' lost.
"Yo're a good hill-billy, but yuh've been bossed."

So I went to congratulate old man Dan,
— But he put his fiddle into my han' —
An' then the noise of the crowd began.

Stephen Vincent Benét

LUCID INTERVAL

WHAT were you saying while we sat
Closed in the crowded motorbus?
Forgive me.   I was looking at
A silver infant octopus.
My brain chose oddly to supply,
Along this winter-smothered street,
A certain morning in July
When, through a rent in opal heat,
I watched a fisherman with spear
Probing the bright Ligurian sea.
He paused and plunged, then hoisted sheer
And waved a wriggling star at me.
Upon the weapon, dangling bare,
It danced in ecstasy of pain
And whipped into the torrid air
A ring of splintered ruby-rain.
And down the fellow's thighs, all wet,
The morning glued a golden vine . . .
But you were saying?   I forget.
The fault was wholly mine.

George O'Neil

TO BARBARY I HAVE NOT SAILED

To Barbary I have not sailed
   By any ship, but yet I know
In Barbary are crystal trees
   Whereon great stars, like apples, grow.

And when by morn's awaking breath
   To chiming life the boughs are stirred,
A silver fire of music shakes
   To raptured song each drowsing bird.

In Barbary by light of moon
   Tall gold and scarlet toadstools dance
Around a pearl-white princess laid
   Forever in a cloudy trance.

And time itself is as a song
   That unremembered drifts away,
As drift pale swans along the tides
   That lave the dawn-bright feet of day.

Eleanor Rogers Cox

A ROAD TO FIRENZE

High noon draws near, the hour is meet
For figs and wine, and rest from heat —
But I have other bread to eat!

An olive bough leans over the wall,
   Its leaves are grey as the old grey stone;
There's heavy dust on the wall and tree
   And the Florentine road I walk alone.

But oh, it's the dust of Italy
   That's turned to gold with this southern sun!
And I am treading it — even I —
   As Dante and Donatello have done!

Here went Raphael in this dust,
   Michelangelo knew this road —
And only a stone's throw past this wall
   The Dukes of Firenze once abode.

What then is the heat and dust to me,
With a Medici wall and an olive tree
In the heart of Tuscan Italy?

Agnes Kendrick Gray

SYRACUSE

AND here where all is waste and wild
Worn cliffs resounding with the seas
And moors where rocks like hoar-frost lie
And hills that know no trees,

There comes a delicacy of flowers
And every turn and twist of breeze
Brings almond petals drifting down
To lakes of deep anemones.

And still beside old temple walls
The goats go browsing at their ease
With asphodels about their horns
And daisies round their knees.

And white and fresh and wild of scent
Along the coast's immensities
The foam wreaths lie beneath the cliffs
Like garlands from a frieze.

                              Elizabeth J. Coatsworth

LUX ÆTERNA

THERE will, of course, be other perfect days,
And crystal sunset clouds again will glow
In windless glory; once more I shall gaze
In wonder while the silent waters flow.
Because this breathless peace does not endure,
I do not weep; the punctual seasons send
Time and again this calm; such gifts secure
This incidental darkness cannot end.
No fleeting magic this, but ordered, clear,

Ever renewed the twilight fires will burn,
And I live lightly sure that year to year
These fragile deathless colors will return,
  Yet now that all the radiance has passed,
  I sigh as though this day had been the last.

                                Irwin Edman

UNCONCERN

THISTLES there are, and thwarted thyme,
And a lonely tree with a looted lime,
And stinkweed running everywhere:
I shall pretend I do not care.
In this small chaos I shall learn
To wear a cloak of unconcern,
Falsely to pin red pimpernel
With a nagging thorn to my lapel.
Only — forgive me if I pause
And wipe two tears with spiders' gauze
For the sake of spring and flowered pear
—Not that I care, not that I care!

                                Virginia Moore

OF A CHILD THAT HAD FEVER

      I BID you, mock not Eros
        Lest Eros mock with you.
      His is a hot distemper
        That hath no feverfew.

      Love, like a child in sickness,
        Brilliant, languid, still,
      In fiery weakness lying,
        Accepts, and hath no will.

See, in that warm dispassion
    Less grievance than surprise,
And pitiable brightness
    In his poor wandering eyes.

Oh delicate heat and madness,
    Oh lust unnerved and faint:
Sparkling in veins and fibers,
    Division and attaint!

I bid you, mock not Eros;
    He knows not doubt or shame,
And, unaware of proverbs,
    The burnt child craves the flame.

Christopher Morley

ELAINE

Oh, come again to Astolat!
    I will not ask you to be kind.
And you may go when you will go,
    And I will stay behind.

I will not say how dear you are,
    Or ask you if you hold me dear,
Or trouble you with things for you
    The way I did last year.

So still the orchard, Lancelot,
    So very still the lake shall be,
You could not guess — though you should guess —
    What is become of me.

So wide shall be the garden-walk,
    The garden-seat so very wide,
You needs must think — if you should think —
    The lily maid had died.

Save that, a little way away,
    I'd watch you for a little while,
To see you speak, the way you speak,
    And smile, — if you should smile.
                        Edna St. Vincent Millay

THIS IS NOT LONELINESS

THIS is not loneliness when we can share
The very foam that beauty breaks into
If the wave leans too far, when all we do
Brings us the same delight, the same despair.
Though we are lost like music and the air
Forgets us, we were music once.   I knew
Just now your voice again, I saw with you
The storm run down a darkening lilac stair.
It is all ours . . . this broken ocean is ours,
The squalls of rain on my side, trailing squalls,
The tawny-ankled Cornish cliffs on yours,
Your thin mauve cloud, your cloudy-pale sand-flowers
Below Tintagel's epic of old walls.
We are not lonely while a dream endures.
                        Grace Hazard Conkling

SONG

BECAUSE I love, I weep,
    Because I grieve, I sing:
Of all things, only sleep
    Is a desired thing.

Denied or given, deep
    Love thrusts its poisoned sting.
Of all things, only sleep
    Is a desired thing.
                        Mary Carolyn Davies

SOMEWHERE I CHANCED TO READ

SOMEWHERE I chanced to read how love may die
From too large giving; so I mused thereon:
"Haply in this our utmost fear should lie?"
And mindful of this caution, I read on;
Then saw these words: "Yet love may equally
Abate through long neglect."   But thereupon
I smiled, believing hereof we were free
And would be ever till our days were done.
Now love is dead, but how I cannot tell —
Whether from too large giving, or neglect.
First dimmed the flame, and after that there fell
The fated silence.   Yet I should elect
Neither of these as cause, but say love died
Out of a cold and calculating pride.

Gustav Davidson.

BY THE WATERS OF BABYLON

By the waters of Babylon by the sea,
On the sand where the waters died,
The sea wind and the tide
Drowned the words you spoke to me.

The sea fell at our feet.   The sand
Hushed the whispering waters, near
The babble of boats by the pier
Was the ictus to the roar on the strand.

By the waters of Babylon a grief to be,
The waiting ships in the bay,
Awed the words we would say
Against the sound of the sea:

For France was below the waters, and the west
Behind me where the rains
Come in November on the window panes,
And the blast shakes the ruined nest

Under the dripping eaves.   What then remains
But memory of the waters of Babylon,
And the ships like swan after swan,
Under the drone of angry hydroplanes?

By the waters of Babylon we did not weep,
Though love comes and is gone,
As the wind is, as waters drawn
In spray from the deep.

Neither for things foreseen and ominous,
For newer hands that somewhere wait
To thrill afresh, the reblossomed fate
Did we surrender dolorous . . .

Change now is yours beyond the waters, nights
Of waiting and of doubt have dimmed desire,
Our hands are calm before the dying fire
Of lost delights.

Babylon by the sea knows us no more.
Between the surge's hushes,
When on the sand the water rushes,
There is no voice of ours upon the shore.

Edgar Lee Masters

BY THE GRAY SEA

WHERE the gray sea lay sad and vast
    You turned your head away,
And we sat silently at last —
    There was no word to say:

> *By the thunder,*
> *By the iron thunder of the sea.*

We could not speak, for the lost hope
  Of the glad days before;
We sat beside the long sea-slope,
  Watching the endless shore —

> *By the thunder,*
> *By the iron thunder of the sea.*

So that, as in the old despair,
  I reached you pleading hands;
But you sat pale and helpless there,
  Beside the barren sands:

> *By the thunder,*
> *By the iron thunder of the sea.*
>   *John Hall Wheelock*

SONG

Though your little word is light,
  Light as any leaf,
Yet it bears a terrible
  Heaviness of grief.

Have I not upon a pool
  Seen how a leaf flits,
Shattering and splintering
  Heaven into bits?

Louis Ginsberg

NOW THAT THESE TWO

Now that these two have parted, let a word
Be said for the yellow
Bird that flew, and the billow
That broke on the sand, and the tree in which they
     heard
The patient wind consent
To all they said, and meant.

These will endure, even after his fashion the bird.
How exquisite is man and how unique,
How strangely strident, how oblique
From nature's habit, who can look unstirred
Upon the earth with veiled eye,
And walk, and talk, and inly die.

Now that these two have parted, it may be said
Perhaps, that they were right;
Something took flight;
And now one sees no raven bringing bread.
The sea has storms, whose shock
Loosens the lichen from the rock.

James Rorty

BRIDAL NIGHT

A Woman Speaks

WHEN darkness was three hours beyond its noon,
Seeing that you lay bound in sleep's duress,
I rose and wandered with a grieving moon
The night's illimitable loneliness,
And felt the ache of that remote distress
Mix with mine own as sorrow weds a tune;
— Far off the dawn approached, the pitiless
Remembering dawn that ever comes too soon.

May Love forgive, may Love keep faith with me,
Who was so false to many a love ere this!
When the dim daybreak glimmers on your face
I shall be sharply stricken of memory:
A risen ghost will claim me in your place,
A dead mouth smile and slay me with a kiss.

Don Marquis

DROWNED WOMAN

He shall be my jailer
Who sets me free
From shackles frailer
Than the wind-spun sea.

He shall be my teacher
Who cries "Be brave,"
To a weeping creature
In a glass-walled wave.

But he shall be my brother
Whose mocking despair
Dives headlong to smother
In the weeds of my hair.

Elinor Wylie

THE LADDER

I had a sudden vision in the night —
I did not sleep, I dare not say I dreamed —
Beside my bed a pallid ladder gleamed
And lifted upward to the sky's dim height:
And every rung shone strangely in that light,

And every rung a woman's body seemed,
Outstretched, and down the sides her long hair
        streamed,
And you — you climbed that ladder of delight!

You climbed, sure-footed, naked rung by rung,
Clasped them and trod them, called them by their
        name,
And my name too I heard you speak at last;
You stood upon my breast the while and flung
A hand up to the next! And then — oh shame —
I kissed the foot that bruised me as it passed.

                                    Leonora Speyer

CHOICE

I SET on this barren board
    (Yours is the choice, not mine)
The bread and leeks for your hunger's ease,
    The unacknowledged wine.

No protests — no demands —
    Always there shall be
The driftwood fire that warms your hands,
    The stars you will not see.

                                    Muna Lee

ULYSSES RETURNS

I

PENELOPE SPEAKS

ULYSSES has come back to me again!
I listen when he tells me of the sea,
But he has strange reserves . . . and strangely he
Stares in the fire . . . I question him, and then
He tells me more of arms . . . and men —

But there is something. . . . *Heart, what can it be*
He sees there that he will not tell to me?
What swift withdrawal makes him alien?
Oh, there are many things that women known,
That no one tells them, no one needs to tell;
And that they know, their dearest never guess!
Because the woman heart is fashioned so.
I know that he has loved another well,
Still his remembering lips know her caress!

II

CIRCE SPEAKS

So swift to bloom, so soon to pass, Love's flower!
The sea that brought him, took him back again —
Ah, well, so is the world and so are men!
But he was happy with me here an hour,
Or almost happy, here within my bower!
He had his silences, his moments when
A strange abstraction took him . . . *I knew then*
That he remembered . . . slipped beyond my power!
I brought him strange, bright blossoms that were
            grown
In emerald gardens, underneath the sea,
We rode white horses, far beyond the shore —
I would not let him sit and think alone!
One day he held me long and tenderly . . .
I knew, I knew that he would come no more!

III

ULYSSES SPEAKS

Was it **I**, was it **I** who dallied there
With a strange, sweet woman beside the sea?
Did she race the wind on the beach with me?

Was it I who kissed her and called her fair?
Was it I who fondled her soft, gold hair —
While she wove and waited me patiently
The woman I love, my Penelope?
Was it I who lingered in Circe's snare?
Now my foot again in my hall is set,
And my keel is dry and my sails are furled:
Beside me, the face I could not forget,
That called me back from across the world —
But there in the fire . . . those red lips wet,
And that soft, gold hair by the sea-mist curled!

IV

PENELOPE SEWS

Oh, the hearts of men, they are rovers, all!
And men will go down to the sea in ships,
And they stop when they hear the sirens call,
And lean to the lure of their red, wet lips!
But never a Circe has snared one yet,
In a green, cool cavern beside the sea,
Who could make the heart of him quite forget
A patiently waiting Penelope!
Yet — there's never a roving one returns
But will sit him down in his easy chair,
While Penelope sews and the fire burns,
And into the depths of it stare . . . and stare.
The fire burns and Penelope sews . . .
He never tells — *but Penelope knows!*

Roselle Mercier Montgomery

THE BEATEN PATH

DIDO with the driven hair
And with the salt sea-spray
Upon those undesired lips
And eyes that follow fading ships, —
It is no use to wander there
Along the shore
All day,
Or hope to see him any more: —
The way
He went is the old way!

Calypso, let the wanderer go
And weave your web and sing your song; —
You knew you could not hold him long,
Though lost and shipwrecked on those shores;
And how can curses keep him yours
When kisses could not make him so?
There is no help from winds that blow;
No seas so strange or so unkind
That they can make him stay behind; —
The way he came he does not know,
But there's one way they all can find!

Fond Simaetha, turning, turning
The bird upon your wheel, and burning
Laurel leaves and barley grain, —
It will not draw him back again.
The moon above the lemon-tree
Will watch with you, but watch in vain;
Nor are the dead of Hecate
Gone more utterly than he; —
Fled along a pathway fleet,
Worn smooth by many feet!

They make a long procession, sweeping
Relentlessly
Through all the past,
Those hearts that were not meant for keeping
And failed too fast.
And ships with windy sails at sea,
And flowery lanes in Sicily
Alike led lovers down the track
That knows no turning back.

Anne Goodwin Winslow

NEVER WILL YOU HOLD ME

NEVER will you hold me
    With puddings and cake
Or even the threat
    Of a heart to break.

Never will you hold me
    With knife, fork, and spoon
As long as the road lies
    Under the moon.

Nor phantoms at fireside
    With grief in the room,
Nor obvious candles
    To jewel the gloom.

But a song satyr-footed,
    A mood of gowns of gold,
And laughter like a wine-cup —
    These things hold.

A song within a song
   And eyes upon the door —
And you will always hold me
   One day more.
                              Charles Divine

CEASE NOT TO BE A MYSTERY

CEASE not to be a mystery to me
Lest I in terror should forsake you quite,
Having more wonder in a cloud at night
Or the vague trembling shadow of a tree.

In shadows or in stones is sure to be
Magic unsquandered — never sold to sight;
Beneath the leaden hilltop some strange might
Secures itself, though I delve endlessly.

Alas, then, if I strive and if I win
To where you are — O let your steady grace
Withhold itself, though I be pledged to follow :
Give up no depth, let no wild word begin —
Lest even love show too distinct a face,
And his enchanting heart look hollow, hollow.
                              Roberta Teale Swartz

THE WISE WOMAN

HIS eyes grow hot, his words grow wild;
   He swears to break the mold and leave her.
She smiles at him as at a child
   That's touched with fever.

She smoothes his ruffled wings, she leans
   To comfort, pamper and restore him;
And when he sulks or scowls, she preens
   His feathers for him.

He hungers after stale regrets,
   Nourished by what she offers gaily;
And all he thinks he never gets
   She feeds him daily.

He lusts for freedom; cries how long
   Must he be bound by what controlled him!
Yet he is glad the chains are strong,
   And that they hold him.

She knows he feels all this, but she
   Is far too wise to let him know it;
He needs to nurse the agony
   That suits a poet.

He laughs to see her shape his life,
   As she half-coaxes, half-commands him;
And groans it's hard to have a wife
   Who understands him.
                 Louis Untermeyer

VALENTINE TO ONE'S WIFE

HEARTS and darts and maids and men,
   Vows and valentines, are here;
Will you give yourself again,
   Love me for another year?

They who give themselves forever,
   All contingencies to cover,
Know but once the kind and clever
   Strategies of loved and lover.

Rather let the year renew
　　Rituals of happiness;
When the season comes to woo,
　　Let me ask, and you say yes.

Love me for another year!
　　Here is heaven enough to climb,
If we measure, now and here,
　　Each delicious step of time.
                                      John Erskine

THE DAY WILL COME

I LAUGH with you because I dare not cry,
And all my words are fluttering and aloof —
Soldiers who know too well that they must die
Will laugh and say that they are bullet-proof.
Will laugh as they go marching forth, knowing
Too well the day will come when no device
Of blowing banners or of bugles blowing
Will obviate their final sacrifice.
The day will come! . . . O dearest, let us climb
The circling stairs up to our little room,
And lay a banquet for the Ogre Time,
And light tall candles for the coming gloom,
And close the windows lest along the street
Familiar steps should sound like marching feet.
                                      Marion Strobel

CONAN OF FORTINGALL

WHY weep you, Conan of Fortingall,
Ere yet the sun be out of his bed?
For that I drank love's brew grown bitter,
When the rose of the moon was red.

What matters it, Conan of Fortingall,
The tassels dance on the laughing corn!
This heart shall dance no more, good mother,
With the minstrel-lark of the morn.

Then drink you, Conan of Fortingall,
Sharp wine as a toast to the lusty day!
The wine's not made by men, sweet mother,
Can drown these dreams away.

I've meat for you, Conan of Fortingall,
And the cakes turn brown as the leaves in the sun —
'Twere better you cut me a shroud, old mother,
For my banqueting days are done.

What mean you, Conan of Fortingall,
With wild talk thick on your wavering breath?
No more, no less, that I slew — ay, mother,
Last night my lass to death.

Let the lass be, Conan of Fortingall —
You've a spear and an ax, and the she-boars wait —
My trail is the unknown trail — yea, mother,
My last hour groweth late.

Is't the *Black Cup*, Conan of Fortingall,
That breaks the belly-band clean in twain?
Even so, and the shadows mass, O mother,
On the stormy crags of pain.

Then night creeps, Conan of Fortingall,
On our six dead eyes in the pale moon's shine;
'Tis well: for love did I kill, old mother,
Your love, and hers, and mine.

                              J. Corson Miller

STEEL

THIS man is dead.
Everything you can say
Is now quite definitely said:
This man held up his head
And had his day,
Then turned his head a little to one way
And slept instead.

Young horses give up their pride:
You break them in
By brief metallic discipline
And something else beside . . .
So this man died.

While he lived I did not know
This man; I never heard
His name.   Now that he lies as though
He were remembering some word
He had forgotten yesterday or so,
It seems a bit absurd
That his blank lids and matted hair should grow
Suddenly familiar. . . .   Let him be interred.

Steady now. . . .   That was his wife
Making that small queer inarticulate sound
Like a knife;
Steady there. . . .   Let him slip easy into the ground;
Do not look at her,
She is fighting for breath. . . .
She is a foreigner. . . .
Polak . . . like him . . . she cannot understand . . .
It is hard . . . leave her alone with death
And a shovelful of sand.

"O the pity of it, the pity of it, Iago!" . . .
Christ, what a hell
Is packed into that line! Each syllable
Bleeds when you say it. . . . No matter: Chicago
Is a far cry from Cracow;
And anyhow
What have Poles
To do with such extraneous things as hearts and souls?

There is nothing here to beat the breast over,
Nothing to relish the curious,
Not a smell of the romantic; this fellow
Was hardly your yearning lover
Frustrated; no punchinello;
But just a hunky in a steel mill. Why then fuss
Because his heavy Slavic face went yellow
With the roaring furnace dust? Now that he is in
The cool sweet crush of dirt, to hell with your sobbing
         violin,
Your sanctimonious cello!
Let the mill bellow!

If you have ever had to do with steel:
The open-hearth, the booming-mill, the cranes
Howling under a fifty-ton load, trains
Yowling in the black pits where you reel
Groggily across a sluice of orange fire, a sheet
Tongued from the conduits that bubble blue green; if
Ever you have got a single whiff
Out of the Bessemer's belly, felt the drag
And drip and curdle of steel spit hissing against hot
         slag;
If ever you have had to eat
One hundred and thirty degrees of solid heat,

Then screwed the hose to the spigot, drowned in
  steam,
Darted back when the rods kicked up a stream
Of fluid steel and had to duck the ladle that slobbered
  over, and scream
Your throat raw to get your "Goddam!" through —
Then I am talking to you.

Steve did that for ten years with quiet eyes
And body down to the belt caked wet
With hardening cinder splash and stiffening sweat
And whatever else there is that clots and never utterly
  dries;
He packed the mud and dolomite, made back-wall,
Herded the heat, and placed his throw in tall
Terrible arcs behind smoked glasses, and watched it
  fall
Heavy and straight and true,
While the blower kept the gas at a growl and the brew
Yelled red and the melter hollered "Heow!" and
  you raveled
Her out and the thick soup gargled and you traveled
Like the devil to get out from under. . . . Well,
  Steve
For ten years of abdominal heft and heave
Worked steel. So much for that. And after
Ten years of night shifts, fourteen hours each,
The Bessemers burn your nerves up, bleach
Rebellion out of your bones; and laughter
Sucked clean out of your guts becomes
More dead than yesterday's feet moving to yesterday's
  drums. . . .
And so they called him "Dummy." The whole gang
From pit-boss down to the last mud-slinger cursed

And squirted tobacco juice in a hot and mixed
    harangue
Of Slovene, Serb, Dutch, Dago, Russian, and —
    worst —
English as hard and toothless as a skull.
And Steve stared straight ahead of him and his eyes
    were dull.

Anna was Steve's little woman
Who labored bitterly enough
Making children of stern and tragic stuff
And a rapture that was hammered rough,
Spilling steel into their spines, yet keeping them wist-
    ful and human. . . .
Anna had her work to do
With cooking and cleaning
And washing the window curtains white as new,
Washing them till they wore through :
For her the white curtains had a meaning —
And starching them white against the savage will
Of the grim dust belching incessantly out of the
    mill ;
Soaking and scrubbing and ironing against that gritty
    reek
Until her head swam and her knees went weak
And she could hardly speak —
A terrible unbeaten purpose persisted :
Color crying against a colorless world !
White against black at the windows flung up, unfurled !
Candles and candle light !
The flags of a lonely little woman twisted
Out of her hunger for cool clean beauty, her hunger
    for white ! —
These were her banners and this was her fight !

No matter how tired she was, however she would ache
In every nerve, she must boil the meat and bake
The bread — and the curtains must go up white for
     Steve's sake!
One thing was certain:

That John and Stanley and Helen and Mary and the
     baby Steven
Must be kept out of the mills and the mill life, even
If it meant her man and she would break
Under the brunt of it: she had talked it through with
     him
A hundred times. . . . Let her eyeballs split, her
     head swim —
The window must have its curtain!

Lately Steve had stopped talking altogether
When he slumped in with his dinner pail and heavily
Hunched over his food —
So Anna and the children let him be;
She was afraid to ask him any why or whether
As he sat with his eyes glued
On vacancy —
So Anna and the children let him brood.
Only sometimes he would suddenly look at them and
     her
In a ghastly fixed blur
Till a vast nausea of terror and compassion stood
Blundering in her heart and swarming in her blood —
And she shivered and knew somehow that it was not
     good.

And then it happened: Spring had come
Like the silver needle-note of a fife,

Like a white plume and a green lance and a glittering
    knife
And a jubilant drum.
But Steve did not hear the earth hum :
Under the earth he could feel merely the fever
And the shock of roots of steel forever;
April had no business with the pit
Or the people — call them people — who breathed in
    it.
The mill was Steve's huge harlot and his head
Lay between breasts of steel on a steel bed,
Locked in a steel sleep and his hands were riveted.

And then it happened : nobody could tell whose
Fault it was, but a torrent of steel broke loose,
Trapped twenty men in the hot frothy mess. . . .
After a week, more or less,
The company, with appropriate finesse,
Having allowed the families time to move,
Expressed a swift proprietary love
By shoving the dump of metal and flesh and shoes
And cotton and cloth and felt
Back into the furnace to remelt.

And that was all, though a dispatch so neat,
So wholly admirable, so totally sweet,
Could not but stick in Steve's dulled brain :
And whether it was the stink or the noise or just plain
Inertia combined with heat,
Steve, one forenoon, on stark deliberate feet,
Let the charging-machine's long iron finger beat
The side of his skull in. . . . There was no pain.

For one fierce instant of unconsciousness
Steve tasted the incalculable caress;

For one entire day he slept between
Sheets that were white and cool, embalmed and clean;
For twenty-four hours he touched the hair of death,
Ran his fingers through it, and it was a deep dark
        green —
And he held his breath.

This man is dead.
Everything you can say
Is now quite definitely said.

                              Joseph Auslander

THE LYRIC DEED

WE sighed and said, The world's high purpose falters;
Here in the West, the human hope is sold;
Behold, our cities are but monstrous altars
That reek in worship to the Beast of Gold!

Now no rapt silence hears the bard intoning;
Our lurid stacks paint out the ancient awe,
And lock-step millions to the motor's moaning
Are herded into Moloch's yawning maw.

With men we stoke our diabolic fires;
Of smithied hearts the soaring steel is made
To dwarf and darken all our godward spires
With drunken towers of Trade.

We said it, blinded with the sweat of duty,
And now, behold! emerging from the dark,
Winged with the old divinity of beauty,
Our living dream mounts morning like a lark!

Of common earth men wrought it, and of wonder;
With lightning have men bitted it and shod;

The throat of it is clothed with singing thunder —
And Lindbergh rides with God!

We have not known, but surely now we know it;
Not thus achieve venality and greed:
The dreaming doer is the master poet —
And lo, the perfect lyric in a deed!

The sunset and the world's new morning hear it;
Ecstatic in the rhythmic motor's roar,
Not seas shall sunder now the human spirit,
For space shall be no more!

John G. Neihardt

UPSTREAM

THE strong men keep coming on.
They go down shot, hanged, sick, broken.
They live on fighting, singing, lucky as plungers.
The strong mothers pulling them on. . . .
The strong mothers pulling them from a dark sea, a
     great prairie, a long mountain.
Call hallelujah, call amen, call deep thanks.
The strong men keep coming on.

Carl Sandburg

THE FIELD OF GLORY

WAR shook the land where Levi dwelt,
And fired the dismal wrath he felt,
That such a doom was ever wrought
As his, to toil while others fought;
To toil, to dream — and still to dream,
With one day barren as another;
To consummate, as it would seem,
The dry despair of his old mother.

Far off one afternoon began
The sound of man destroying man;
And Levi, sick with nameless rage,
Condemned again his heritage,
And sighed for scars that might have come,
And would, if once he could have sundered
Those harsh, inhering claims of home
That held him while he cursed and wondered.

Another day, and then there came,
Rough, bloody, ribald, hungry, lame,
But yet themselves, to Levi's door,
Two remnants of the day before.
They laughed at him and what he sought;
They jeered him, and his painful acre;
But Levi knew that they had fought
And left their manners to their Maker.

That night, for the grim widow's ears,
With hopes that hid themselves in fears,
He told of arms, and fiery deeds,
Whereat one leaps the while he reads,
And said he'd be no more a clown,
While others drew the breath of battle. —
The mother looked him up and down,
And laughed — a scant laugh with a rattle.

She told him what she found to tell,
And Levi listened, and heard well
Some admonitions of a voice
That left him no cause to rejoice. —
He sought a friend, and found the stars,
And prayed aloud that they should aid him;
But they said not a word of wars,
Or of a reason why God made him.

And who's of this or that estate
We do not wholly calculate,
When baffling shades that shift and cling
Are not without their glimmering;
When even Levi, tired of faith,
Beloved of none, forgot by many,
Dismissed as an inferior wraith,
Reborn may be as great as any.

Edwin Arlington Robinson

OLD TIMERS

I AM an ancient reluctant conscript.
On the soup wagons of Xerxes I was a cleaner of pans.
On the march of Miltiades' phalanx I had a haft and
  head;
I had a bristling gleaming spear-handle.

Red-headed Caesar picked me for a teamster.
He said, 'Go to work, you Tuscan bastard,
Rome calls for a man who can drive horses.'

The units of conquest led by Charles the Twelfth,
The whirling whimsical Napoleonic columns:
They saw me one of the horseshoers.

I trimmed the feet of a white horse Bonaparte swept
  the night stars with.
Lincoln said, 'Get into the game; your nation takes
  you.'
And I drove a wagon and team and I had my arm shot
  off
At Spotsylvania Court House.

I am an ancient reluctant conscript.

Carl Sandburg

THE GOOD HOUR

THE man who met a phalanx with their spears
　　And gave his life in one sharp sacrifice,
Knew nothing of the agony of years,
　　Of what man can endure before he dies.

Some men die early and are spared much care,
　　Some suddenly, escaping worse than death;
But he is fortunate who happens where
　　He can exult and die in the same breath.

Louise Driscoll

THE GREY PLUME

THE long heron feather
　　O'Dogherty wore,
Still sweeps o'er the heather
　　But not as before;
And well may the heron
　　Take pride in his plume
With the head of O'Dogherty
　　Red in the tomb.

The valleys are spurning
　　Gay flowers, beneath
The purple of mourning
　　Aloft on the heath;
And well may the sorrow
　　Of Nature be shown,
Though the heron is happy
　　In wild Innishowen.

Bright was the bonnet
　　That guided his men,

But the grey feather on it
      Fell red in the glen;
And well may the Saxon
      Take pride in its fall,
While birds wear their plumage
      Above Donegal.

Ochone, that the feather
      O'Dogherty wore
Should sweep o'er the heather,
      But not as before!
Och! Och! that the heron
      Should fly with grey plume
O'er Cahir O'Dogherty
      Red in his tomb.

                              Francis Carlin

NOT ONLY SWORDS

I PALTERED lately with the strong,
      I gave a fool's assent;
Yes, I unfolded a flag of song
      When the soldiers went.

I honoured liars afterwards,
      Tricking my own shame,
Singing a light upon the swords
      When no light came.

Poets, like soldiers, suffer wrongs
      That are very old:
Not only swords but also songs
      Are bought and sold.

                              Witter Bynner

GRASS

PILE the bodies high at Austerlitz and Waterloo.
Shovel them under and let me work —
> I am the grass; I cover all.

And pile them high at Gettysburg
And pile them high at Ypres and Verdun.
Shovel them under and let me work.
Two years, ten years, and passengers ask the con-
ductor:
> What place is this?
> Where are we now?

> I am the grass.
> Let me work.
> > *Carl Sandburg*

GRAY

MY heart is gray with bird-wings going south on the
    north wind,
Gray with a dark sky leaning on dark water,
My heart is gray with a bare tree standing dumb on
    a hilltop
Between me and a chill evening sky.
I would warm myself with thoughts of white-blos-
    somed cherry-trees
Holding still their white pitchers
For the drip of May moonlight,
I would comfort myself with the memory of the clean
    yellow bowls of May mornings —
But the wind throws itself on the cold road
And a swirl of dead leaves would choke me,
Holding me straight to November.

It's a gray road that goes over the hills,
It's a frozen gray moon that it leads to,
And only a gray heart can make songs for its liking.
Frederick R. McCreary

IMMORTAL

THE last thin acre of stalks that stood
   Was never the end of the wheat,
Always something fled to the wood,
   As if the field had feet.

In front of the sickle something rose —
   Mouse, or weasel, or hare;
We struck and struck, but our worst blows
   Dangled in the air.

Nothing could touch the little soul
   Of the grain.   It ran to cover,
And nobody knew in what warm hole
   It slept till the winter was over,

And early seeds lay cold in the ground.
   Then — but nobody saw —
It burrowed back with never a sound,
   And awoke the thaw.
Mark Van Doren

AUTUMNAL

WINTER wheat is fair to see
Green and trimly groomed,
But oh, it's fallow fields for me
Softly furred and plumed!

Pastures — they are smoothly cropped
By cows and nibbling sheep.
Burdened by their harvest still
The weary cornfields sleep.

Orchards stretch their crooked limbs
Beneath a frosty moon,
And shudder for the lack of leaves
With winter coming soon.

But fallow fields, with mulleins warm
And ferns and shaggy grass,
Drowse like thick-furred animals
And let the season pass.

Marie Emilie Gilchrist

HERBS

A SERVICEABLE thing
Is fennel, mint, or balm,
Kept in the thrifty calm
Of hollows, in the spring;
Or by old houses pent.
Dear is its ancient scent
To folk that love the days forgot,
Nor think that God is not.

Sage, lavender, and rue,
For body's hurt and ill,
For fever and for chill;
Rosemary, strange with dew,
For sorrow and its smart;
For breaking of the heart;
Yet pain, dearth, tears, all come to dust,
As even the herbs must.

Life-everlasting, too,
Windless, poignant, and sere,
That blows in the old year,
Townsmen, for me and you.
Why fret for wafting airs?
Why haste to sell our wares?
Captains and clerks, this shall befall;
This is the end of all.

Oh, this the end indeed!
Oh, unforgotten things,
Gone out of all the springs;
The quest, the dream, the creed!
Gone out of all the lands,
And yet safe in God's hands; —
For shall the dull herbs live again,
And not the sons of men?

Lizette Woodworth Reese

THE SHEAVES

WHERE long the shadows of the wind had rolled,
Green wheat was yielding to the change assigned;
And as by some vast magic undivined
The world was turning slowly into gold.
Like nothing that was ever bought or sold
It waited there, the body and the mind;
And with a mighty meaning of a kind
That tells the more the more it is not told.

So in a land where all days are not fair,
Fair days went on till on another day
A thousand golden sheaves were lying there,

Shining and still, but not for long to stay —
As if a thousand girls with golden hair
Might rise from where they slept and go away.

Edwin Arlington Robinson

ADONIS

I

EACH of us like you
has died once,
each of us like you
has passed through drift of wood-leaves,
cracked and bent
and tortured and unbent
in the winter frost,
then burnt into gold points,
lighted afresh,
crisp amber, scales of gold-leaf,
gold turned and re-welded
in the sun-heat;

each of us like you
has died once,
each of us has crossed an old wood-path
and found the winter leaves
so golden in the sun-fire
that even the live wood-flowers
were dark.

II

Not the gold on the temple-front
where you stand,
is as gold as this,
not the gold that fastens your sandal,

nor the gold reft
through your chiselled locks
is as gold as this last year's leaf,
not all the gold hammered and wrought
and beaten
on your lover's face,
brow and bare breast
is as golden as this:

each of us like you
has died once,
each of us like you
stands apart, like you
fit to be worshipped.

H. D.

ARCTURUS IN AUTUMN

WHEN, in the gold October dusk, I saw you near to
    setting,
  Arcturus, bringer of spring,
Lord of the summer nights, leaving us now in autumn,
  Having no pity on our withering;

Oh then I knew at last that my own autumn was upon
    me,
  I felt it in my blood,
Restless as dwindling streams that still remember
  The music of their flood.

There in the thickening dark a wind-bent tree above
    me
  Loosed its last leaves in flight —
I saw you sink and vanish, pitiless Arcturus,
  You will not stay to share our lengthening night.

Sara Teasdale

SCARS

THE smell of ruin in the autumn air,
  When rusty twilights come too early down,
Will take the hearts of strong men unaware,
  And lure them from the friendly, lighted town, —
To walk old, lonely roadways where they learn
  Again of summers that have come to husk,
Where smoky stars like low-hung lanterns burn
  Above the crumbling borders of the dusk.

On littered ways where leaves are crisp and curled,
  And mist comes in between the passing shapes,
There go the proud and desolate of the world,
  Wrapped in their thoughtful silences like capes,
Walking dark roads beneath the autumn stars,
Each with his hidden and historic scars.

David Morton

I THOUGHT I HAD OUTLIVED MY PAIN

I THOUGHT I had outlived my pain,
  For when, on hurrying feet,
I passed the house that you had known
  Your memory made it sweet.

But when I came to my own door
  Where you had never been
All the old sorrow met me there
  And I could not go in.

Elisabeth Scollard

THE DARK HILLS

Dark hills at evening in the west,
Where sunset hovers like a sound
Of golden horns that sang to rest
Old bones of warriors under ground,
Far now from all the bannered ways
Where flash the legions of the sun,
You fade — as if the last of days
Were fading, and all wars were done.

Edwin Arlington Robinson

AUTUMN IN CARMEL

Now with a sigh November comes to the brooding
land.
Yellowing now toward winter the willows of Carmel
stand.
Under the pine her needles lie redder with the rain.
Gipsy birds from the northland visit our woods again.

Hunters wait on the hillside, watching the plowman
pass
And the red hawk's shadow gliding over the newborn
grass.
Purple and white the sea-gulls swarm at the river-
mouth.
Pearl of mutable heavens towers upon the south.

Westward pine and cypress stand in a sadder light.
Flocks of the veering curlew flash for an instant white.
Wreaths of the mallard, shifting, melt on the vacant
blue.
Over the hard horizon dreams are calling anew.

Dumb with the sense of wonder hidden from hand
and eye, —
Wistful yet for the Secret ocean and earth deny, —
Baffled for Beauty's haunting, hearts are peaceless
to-day,
Seeing the dusk of sapphire deepen within the bay.

Far on the kelp the heron stands for awhile at rest.
The lichen-colored breaker hollows a leaning breast.
Desolate, hard and tawny, the sands lie clean and
wide,
Dry with the wafted sea-wind, wet with the fallen
tide.

Early the autumn sunset tinges to mauve the foam;
Shyly the rabbit, feeding, crosses the road toward
home.
Daylight, lingering golden, touches the tallest tree,
Ere the rain, like silver harp-strings, comes slanting in
from the sea.

George Sterling

"A SOUND OF GOING IN THE TOPS OF THE MULBERRY TREES. . . ."

THERE is a sense of journeying
upon the trees.

So many yellow sails are set —
so many red!

There is a hush that waits
on signals —
a silence leaning toward the moment
when the trees shall sound
and all the leaves flutter and go.

The days gather like colored leaves
upon the hills.

An empty sail unfurls
and fills.

There is a sound of passing —
the bugles of departure blow!

Henry Bellamann

THE FLYING DEAD

THE air was full of withered leaves,
  The golden and the red;
They cried to one who hid his eyes,
  "Follow the flying dead.

"Come loose your soul from off the bough
  Where it doth hang and sigh,
And give it to the long-maned wind
  And see your dead soul fly.

"And loose your heart from off the stem
  Where it doth pulse and pale,
And on the sea of running air
  Let your dead heart sail.

"For only the dead are travellers,"
  The wild leaves sang and said.
"Follow, follow, follow,
  Follow the flying dead!"

Rose O'Neill

MISGIVING

ALL crying "We will go with you, O Wind!"
The foliage follow him, leaf and stem;
But a sleep oppresses them as they go,
And they end by bidding him stay with them.

Since ever they flung abroad in spring
The leaves had promised themselves this flight,
Who now would fain seek sheltering wall,
Or thicket, or hollow place for the night.

And now they answer his summoning blast
With an ever vaguer and vaguer stir,
Or at utmost a little reluctant whirl
That drops them no further than where they were.

I only hope that when I am free
As they are free to go in quest
Of the knowledge beyond the bounds of life
It may not seem better to me to rest.

Robert Frost

SLEEPWARD

ALL things reach up to take the Year's last gift,
Then slowly sleepward drift.
Be not deceived if some charmed bush or hedge
Laugh out, on winter's edge,
Bidding you pluck a flower as you go by,
And trust the yet bland sky.
Be not deceived, the sands are well outrun,
The gala-day is done:
There is no fruit can ripen from a flower
That dares the borrowed hour!
To sleep, to sleep, to sleep, and ask no more
To put within your store;

For, if you have not gathered, 'tis too late —
Swings to, Oblivion's gate.

Be not deceived that yester-evening heard
A flock-abandoned bird.
Against the clear, old-ivory west, sharp-limned,
His broken song he hymned:
But sleep now claims his solitary breast
That was the orchard's guest:
The leaves that loved the bird — they, too, asleep,
His little shape will keep.

Earth sleeps in stillness now, and all of hers,
Obedient vanishers,
Into their chosen cubicles withdrawn,
Stir not at any dawn;
Nor any time unless the wild mice dance,
When the round moon enchants,
Upon a floor polished with frosty fire
And then again retire.
No one will fret or strive to keep awake
But will the feast partake
Of sleep — of sleep-on-sleep, while turns the sphere;
Still here — and yet not here!

Who knows, of us, who heard the sleepward call,
If we be waking all?
If just at one pale moment when the chill
Seemed to o'ercome the will,
We sank not to some deeper blest estate
Where suasive dreams await?
Nor may I know, if me such magic keep
I speak these words in sleep!

Edith M. Thomas

AUTUMN AND DEATH

THEY are coy, these sisters, Autumn and Death,
And they both have learnt what it is to wait.
Not a leaf is jarred by their cautious breath,
The little feather-weight
Petals of climbing convolvulus
Are scarcely even tremulous.

Who hears Autumn moving down
The garden-paths?   Who marks her head
Above the oat-sheaves?   A leaf gone brown
On the ash, and a maple-leaf turned red —
Yet a rose that's freshly blown
Seals your eyes to the change in these,
For it's mostly green about the trees.

And Death with her silver-slippered feet,
Do you hear her walk by your garden-chair?
The cool of her hand makes a tempered heat,
That's all, and the shadow of her hair
Is curiously sweet.
Does she speak?   If so, you have not heard;
The whisper of Death is without a word.

The sisters, Autumn and Death, with strange
Long silences, they bide their time,
Nor ever step beyond the range
Allotted to a pantomime.
But the soundless hours chime,
One after one, and their faces grow
To an altered likeness, slow — slow.

Grim is the face which Autumn turns
To a sky all bare of obscuring leaves,

And her hair is red as a torch where it burns
In the dry hearts of the oaten sheaves.
But Death has a face which yearns
With a gaunt desire upon its prey,
And Death's dark face hides yesterday.

Then Autumn holds her hands to touch
Death's hands, and the two kiss, cheek by cheek,
And one smiles to the other, and the smiles say much,
And neither one has need to speak.
Two gray old sisters, such
Are Autumn and Death when their tasks are done,
And their world is a world where a blackened sun
Shines like ebony over the floes
Of a shadeless ice, and no wind blows.

Amy Lowell

THE ENDURING

If the autumn ended
Ere the birds flew southward,
If in the cold with weary throats
They vainly strove to sing,
Winter would be eternal;
Leaf and bush and blossom
Would never once more riot
In the spring.

If remembrance ended
When life and love are gathered,
If the world were not living
Long after one is gone,
Song would not ring, nor sorrow
Stand at the door in evening;
Life would vanish and slacken,
Men would be changed to stone.

But there will be autumn's beauty
Dropping upon our weariness,
There will be hopes unspoken
And joys to haunt us still;
There will be dawn and sunset
Though we have cast the world away,
And the leaves dancing
Over the hill.

John Gould Fletcher

THE HAWTHORN TREE

THE hawthorn tree is strange in May,
Dense with her buds. I cannot say
What death, what legend, what old dream,
What shadowiness of longing seem
Risen throughout her, subtle, slow,
Into the blossom from the bough.

But she is deep in winter now.
By day the sunlit smoke of snow
Blows over her, and glazed at night
She glitters, star and thorn alight.
Her thrill is cold; her secret myth
Held in the sap she slumbers with.

Roberta Teale Swartz

SNOWFALL

AT noon the elfin flakes began to fall.
  The air was intricate with such a flight
Of unsubstantial bloom as left on all
  The earth a lovely petaling of light.

A wide swift radiance dazzled earth and air ;
  There was no rich disguise, no gold to mar
The hushed and heaping whiteness anywhere
  Till all the city was a silver star.

(*And in our loneliness and pride we said,*
  This is that city gained in one lost breath,
The many-petaled city of the dead —
  Those are the muted corridors of death.)

Now noon went out in white, and we who feared
  The ebbing tide of day, the loss of light,
Watched how the subtle wings of twilight veered
  In blue obscurities until the bright

Curved crystal moon, of carven light and dew
  Wove crystal spells she may not weave well
    twice. . . .
O night of still strange bloom! The white hours
    through
  The star-like city burned, all fire and ice.

(*And in our loneliness and pride we dreamed*
  This was that easeful city pale with rime
Of ancient sleep, where cliffs of silence gleamed
  With hoar of space and drift on drift of time.)
                                    Marjorie Meeker

WHITE FEAR

I AM not afraid in April,
  I am cool enough to pass
Where robins burn like embers
  And tulips scorch the grass.

But oh when snow has fallen
  On a little city park,
I would not dream to venture
  Alone there in the dark!

For if I made one motion
  Along the muffled street,
Whole whitened trees would tumble
  Into ashes at my feet.

The almond lamps would ripen
  In the velvet shell and fall
Upon the plush of pavements
  With no sound at all.

And, trembling in the silence,
  Like someone very old,
I would find my hair silver,
  And feel my heart cold.

               Winifred Welles

IT WILL BE A HARD WINTER

THEY say the blue king jays have flown
From woods of Westchester;
So I to Luthany shall flee,
But I will make no stir;
For who fair Luthany would see
Must set him forth alone.

In screwing winds last night the snow
Creaked like an angry jinn;
And two old men from up the State,
Said "Bears went early in;"
Half pausing by my ice-locked gate;
"March will be late to blow."

So I for Luthany am bound;
But I will take no pack.
You can not find the way, you know,
With feet that leave a track;
But light as blowing leaf must go;
And you must hear a sound

That's like a singing strange and high
Of bird you've never seen;
Then two ghosts come; like doves they move;
While you must walk between;
And one is Youth and one is Love,
Who say "We did not die."

The harp-built walls of Luthany
Are builded high and strong
To shelter singer, fool and seer,
And glad they live and long.
All others die who enter there,
But they are safe, these three.

The seer can warm his body through
By some far fire he sees;
The fool can naked dance in snow;
The singer — as he please!
And which I be of these, Oh ho!
That is a guess for you.

Once in a thousand years, they say,
The walls are beaten down;
And then they find a singer dead,
But swift they set a crown
Upon his lowly careless head,
And sing his song for aye.

So I to Luthany shall flee,
While here the winter raves;
God send I go not as one blind
A-dancing upon graves;
God save a madman if I find
War's heel on Luthany.

Olive Tilford Dargan

STOPPING BY WOODS ON A SNOWY EVENING

WHOSE woods these are I think I know.
His house is in the village though;
He will not see me stopping here
To watch his woods fill up with snow.

My little horse must think it queer
To stop without a farmhouse near
Between the woods and frozen lake
The darkest evening of the year.

He gives his harness bells a shake
To ask if there is some mistake.
The only other sound's the sweep
Of easy wind and downy flake.

The woods are lovely, dark and deep.
But I have promises to keep,
And miles to go before I sleep,
And miles to go before I sleep.

Robert Frost

LUTE AND FURROW

THE winter has grown so still
I can stand at the foot of the hill
Where the stream beneath the bridge
Is dry as a heart after grief,
And hear at the top of the ridge
The wind as it lifts a leaf.

At last there is time, I say;
I will shut out the strife to-day;
I will take up my pen and once more
Meet that stranger, my soul, nor be dumb
As when earth was the whirlwind's floor,
And Life at her loom sat numb.

Springs, many as ever have been,
On sandals of moss shall slip in;
There is time for the laugh we would fling,
For the wiping of dust from our stars,
For a bee on his marketing wing,
For the forester wind's wild wares.

Comes the joy and the rushing pulse
That in beauty's beginning exults;
Then the weight tied fast to the heart;
The doubt that deadens the dawn;
And the raining sting and the smart
Of invisible whips laid on.

Olive Tilford Dargan

FIRST SNOW

THE cows are bawling in the mountains.
Snowflakes fall.
They are leaving the pools and pebbled fountains.
Troubled, they bawl.

They are winding down the mountain's shoulders
Through the open pines,
The wild rose thickets and the granite boulders
In broken lines.
Each calf trots close beside its mother
And so they go,
Bawling and calling to one another
About the snow.

Charles Erskine Scott Wood

SNOW WATER

THEY say snow water is not good to drink.
The snow, between the granite and the suns,
Yields up its vintage.   Crystal-clear it runs,
Lupins and shooting stars on either brink.

But all is sparkling sickness there for men;
Wait while it lashes downward from its birth,
Wearing a rebel way against the earth
Till earth has conquered.   You may drink it then.

But here, where all the rocks are laced with scars
Of old world-wrenching wounds, its silver grips
Stuff that is almost poison to our lips —
Free space, sheer sun, the tempests and the stars.

Frank Ernest Hill

YET NOTHING LESS

THIS is the top.   Here we can only go
Back to the world, that Lilliput below:
A child's toy village scattered in the snow.

What have we come for then? This scornful height
Scarce moved an inch to meet us. Black and white
Seem colder still in this ash-ivory light.

What saves these frozen trees from coming out
And waving threatening arms as though in doubt
Of what it is that we have come about?

What gives these common curves, these hills that
        part
As casually as schoolboys, power to start
Cries from the lips and tears within the heart?

Nothing so much, perhaps, yet nothing less
Than that which wintry earth knows to express —
Love that no longer lives on loveliness.

                                Louis Untermeyer

THE ONSET

ALWAYS the same, when on a fated night
At last the gathered snow lets down as white
As may be in dark woods, and with a song
It shall not make again all winter long
Of hissing on the yet uncovered ground,
I almost stumble looking up and round,
As one who overtaken by the end
Gives up his errand, and lets death descend
Upon him where he is, with nothing done
To evil, no important triumph won,
More than if life had never yet begun.

Yet all the precedent is on my side:
I know that winter death has never tried
The earth but it has failed: the snow may heap

In long storms an undrifted four feet deep
As measured against maple, birch and oak,
It cannot check the peeper's silver croak;
And I shall see the snow all go down hill
In water of a slender April rill
That flashes tail through last year's withered brake
And dead weeds, like a disappearing snake.
Nothing will be left white but here a birch
And there a clump of houses with a church.

Robert Frost

PEACE ON EARTH

The Archer is awake!
The Swan is flying!
Gold against blue
An Arrow is lying.
There is hunting in heaven —
Sleep safe till tomorrow.

The Bears are abroad!
The Eagle is screaming!
Gold against blue
Their eyes are gleaming!
Sleep!
Sleep safe till tomorrow!

The Sisters lie
With their arms intertwining;
Gold against blue
Their hair is shining!
The Serpent writhes!
Orion is listening!
Gold against blue
His sword is glistening!

Sleep!
There is hunting in heaven —
Sleep safe till tomorrow.
                    William Carlos Williams

THE SKATER OF GHOST LAKE

GHOST LAKE'S a dark lake, a deep lake and cold;
Ice black as ebony, frostily scrolled;
Far in its shadows a faint sound whirrs;
Steep stand the sentineled deep, dark firs.

A brisk sound, a swift sound, a ring-tinkle-ring;
Flit-flit, — a shadow, with a stoop and a swing,
Flies from a shadow through the crackling cold.
Ghost Lake's a deep lake, a dark lake and old!

Leaning and leaning, with a stride and a stride,
Hands locked behind him, scarf blowing wide,
Jeremy Randall skates, skates late,
Star for a candle, moon for a mate.

Black is the clear glass now that he glides,
Crisp is the whisper of long lean strides,
Swift is his swaying, — but pricked ears hark.
None comes to Ghost Lake late after dark!

Cecily only, — yes, it is she!
Stealing to Ghost Lake, tree after tree,
Kneeling in snow by the still lake side,
Rising with feet winged gleaming to glide.

Dust of the ice swirls.   Here is his hand.
Brilliant his eyes burn.   Now, as was planned,
Arm across arm twined, laced to his side,
Out on the dark lake lightly they glide.

Dance of the dim moon, a rhythmical reel,
A swaying, a swift tune, — skurr of the steel;
Moon for a candle, maid for a mate,
Jeremy Randall skates, skates late.

Black as if lacquered the wide lake lies;
Breath is a frost-fume, eyes seek eyes;
Souls are a sword-edge tasting the cold.
Ghost Lake's a deep lake, a dark lake and old!

Far in the shadows hear faintly begin
Like a string pluck-plucked of a violin,
Muffled in mist on the lake's far bound,
Swifter and swifter, a low singing sound!

Far in the shadows and faint on the verge
Of blue cloudy moonlight, see it emerge,
Flit-flit, — a phantom, with a stoop and a swing. . .
Ah, it's a night bird, burdened of wing!

Pressed close to Jeremy, laced to his side,
Cecily Culver, dizzy you glide.
Jeremy Randall sweepingly veers
Out on the dark ice far from the piers.

"Jeremy!"   "Sweetheart?"   "What do you fear?"
"Nothing, my darling, — nothing is here!"
"Jeremy?"   "Sweetheart?"   "What do you flee?"
"Something — I know not; something I see!"

Swayed to a swift stride, brisker of pace,
Leaning and leaning they race and they race;
Ever that whirring, that crisp sound thin
Like a string pluck-plucked of a violin;

Ever that swifter and low singing sound
Sweeping behind them, winding them round;
Gasp of their breath now, that chill flakes fret;
Ice black as ebony, — blacker — like jet!

Ice shooting fangs forth — sudden — like spears;
Crackling of lightning, — a roar in their ears!
Shadowy a phantom swerves off from its prey. . . .
No, it's a night bird flit-flits away!

Low-winging moth-owl, home to your sleep!
Ghost Lake's a still lake, a cold lake and deep.
Faint in its shadows a far sound whirrs.
Black stand the ranks of its sentinel firs.

William Rose Benét

HOUND AT NIGHT

I DID not know how brittle
Was the silence
Till quick, shrewd barks of a hound
Pelted over the hills
Breaking the stillness into fragments
Like slivers of bright looking glass.

Louise Ayres Garnett

IF SCARS ARE WORTH THE KEEPING

STEEL, hard to dent, once dented
    Is history of blows
That, by the rust augmented,
    Barren resistance shows —
    And that is all one knows.

O heart I thought to harden
 To steel to bear the blow,
You grew more like a garden
 Time walks and the winds sow —
 And seasons come and go.

The sod, where heels were twisted,
 Springs back at last in rain.
Spots, sometimes flower-misted,
 Some prone earth-pressing pain
 First crushed where it had lain.

If scars are worth the keeping
 The steel is rich indeed —
O heart, this wistful reaping
 Of restless waiting seed
 That flowers where you bleed!
     Glenn Ward Dresbach

THE BUILDER

THE edges of the stones are sharp
But I shall travel far
For I must seek and seek and seek
Wherever such stones are.

I am building me a secret place
With stones that cut my hands,
But I must build and build and build
Until a temple stands.
     Caroline Giltinan

TRIUMPH

My supercilious soul
Looks down on my high joy,
My triumphing,
And murmurs coldly :
You blind thing!

But when my joy has left,
My wakened soul,
Alert for cries bereft,
With lamp and bowl
Flies to me, mothering.

Kathryn White Ryan

AFTER DISASTER

Who hurts his heel upon a stone,
Knows that some trick of life is done;
No longer his the rage to do,
To rush across the hurrying sun.

Such thrift he shows with his new hours
That he spares one, to stoop his head
To some grey book he read with her
Who loved him long since.   She is dead.

Lovely, secure, unhastening things
Fast-kept for this, grip as of yore; —
The drowsy traffic of the bees;
The scarlet haws beyond a door.

Lizette Woodworth Reese

BITTER-SWEET

ONCE when a child I ran to pick
  Sprays of these berries bright,
To hang them high about the hall
  Like lanterns all alight.

But, ah, to-day I never go
  Along the windy lane,
My house is full of Bitter-Sweet —
  I need not pluck again!

Elisabeth Scollard

I SHALL BE LOVED AS QUIET THINGS

I SHALL be loved as quiet things
Are loved — white pigeons in the sun,
Curled yellow leaves that whisper down
One after one;

The silver reticence of smoke
That tells no secret of its birth
Among the fiery agonies
That turn the earth;

Cloud-islands; reaching arms of trees;
The frayed and eager little moon
That strays unheeded through a high
Blue afternoon.

The thunder of my heart must go
Under the muffling of the dust —
As my gray dress has guarded it
The grasses must;

For it has hammered loud enough,
Clamored enough, when all is said:
Only its quiet part shall live
When I am dead.

Karle Wilson Baker

WE ARE OLD

WE are old — it must be so,
Oft they say it — they who know.
Care they not what we could tell!
Age with age companions well:
Walk a little way with me,
Talk, if so it pleases thee,
Talk of that which is — or seems!
If we both fall into dreams
So the rest is never told,
Does it matter?   We are old.

Walk a little way with me —
Short enough the way will be:
One of us, some time, shall start,
Finding more than dreams depart.
Round the lone one then will fold
Deeper shadows.   We are old.

Edith M. Thomas

TOO SOON THE LIGHTEST FEET

Too soon the lightest feet are lead,
All tongues of silver cease;
Will Shakespeare with a word half said
Is pledged to hold his peace!

So artlessly kings fall asleep,
Wearing their crowns awry,
Their hands forget what they would keep
And loosen as they lie.

And lovers, mellow to the sound
Of meadow larks in Spring,
Grow inattentive underground,
Nor heed them when they sing.

I dare not say my joy is great
Time presses on me so,
Counting the early hour as late
What space I have to go,

But faint for rapture like the rest
Life chooses so to mock,
Speechless, I hold love to my breast
And listen to the clock!

Amanda Benjamin Hall

WHEN I AM OLD

WHEN I am old and you are young
　Who died so long ago,
I'll say, "A fool I was to mourn,
　But how was I to know?

"A fool I was to mourn, my dear,
　The fortune that you had;
Now here am I grown gray, while you
　Will always be a lad."

When I am old the things I say
Perhaps will then be true,
Since fire and faith of me to-day
Lie young and lost with you.
Marjorie Meeker

OLD WOMEN

OLD women sit, stiffly, mosaics of pain,
Framed in drab doorways looking on the dark.
Rarely they rouse to gossip or complain
As dozing bitches break their dream to bark.
And then once more they fold their creaking bones
In silence, pulled about them like a shawl.
Their memories: a heap of tumbling stones,
Once builded stronger than a city wall.
Sometimes they mend the gaps with twitching hand —
Because they see a woman big with child,
Because a wet wind smells of grave-pocked land,
Because a train wailed, because troops defiled.
Sometimes old women limp through altered streets
Whose hostile houses beat them down to earth;
Now in their beds they fumble at the sheets
That once were spread for bridal, once for birth,
And now are laid for women who are cold
With difficult plodding and with sitting still.
Old women, pitying all that age can kill,
Lie quiet, wondering that they are old.
Babette Deutch

HORIZONS

YET we have felt some ecstasy in time,
And we have seen much loveliness in space,
And we have known hours when the veil
Was parted from the hid and perfect face.

And water waits on thirst, on famine food,
For weariness is sleep, and all the dry
Burning and level deserts end in hills
That climb with cups of crystal to the sky.

Struthers Burt

COME, CAPTAIN AGE

COME, Captain Age,
With your great sea-chest full of treasure!
Under the yellow and wrinkled tarpaulin
Disclose the carved ivory
And the sandalwood inlaid with pearl:
Riches of wisdom and years.
Unfold the India shawl
With its border of emerald and orange and crimson
    and blue,
Weave of a lifetime!
I shall be rich and splendid
With the spoils of the Indies of Age.

Sarah N. Cleghorn

SPINNERS AT WILLOWSLEIGH

THE old women sit at Willowsleigh and spin,
And sing and shout above the humming din.

They are so very old, and brown and wise,
One is afraid to look them in the eyes.

Their bony fingers make a crackling sound,
Like dead bones shaking six feet underground,

Their toothless singing mocks; it seems to say:
"What I was yesterday, you are to-day.

"Stars kissed our eyes, the sunlight loved our brow,
You'll be tomorrow, lass, what we are now."

They sing and talk, they are so old and lean;
And the whole earth is young, and fresh, and green.

Once they were flowers, and flame and living bread;
Now they are old and brown and all but dead.

Marya Zaturensky

THE CROWS

THE woman who has grown old
And knows desire must die,
Yet turns to love again,
Hears the crows' cry.

She is a stem long hardened,
A weed that no scythe mows,
The heart's laughter will be to her
The crying of the crows,

Who slide in the air with the same voice
Over what yields not and what yields,
Alike in spring, or when there is only bitter
Winter burning in the fields.

Louise Bogan

BALLAD OF THREAD FOR A NEEDLE

I HAD walked a long way
By the end of afternoon,
My lone path crossed
The bare old dune;

A shining needle
  Was buried in my breast,
It was sharp, it was empty,
  And I had no rest.

The sand grew gray
  As I walked along,
The sky grew dim
  And the light seemed wrong.

Then far to the right
  I saw an old woman;
"It's good," I said,
  "To see something human!"

She was gray as the dune,
  Then I saw her clearer;
She was walking away
  But she kept coming nearer.

My heart stood still
  And then began to throb
And crowded in my throat
  Like a choking sob;

The sand came alive
  And cried beneath my track;
With crumbling fingers
  It tried to hold me back.

The woman leaned over
  And scooped up sand
That ran between the fingers
  Of her skinny hand.

My heart swelled and quivered
   And like a bubble broke;
I came close and listened
   While the old woman spoke:

"Threads of sand
   On a crumbling spool;
Dreams for a wise man,
   Dreams for a fool,

"Magic thread
   That runs and gleams,
Threads of sand
   That men call dreams.

"With threads of sand
   They sew a shroud
To wrap the heart
   In a dusty cloud,

"A crumbling shroud
   But heavy as lead,
To wrap a heart
   When its dreams lie dead.

"There never was a dream
   That any man stole,
For threads of sand
   You pay your soul!"

"If my soul is money,"
   I heard myself say,
"It's only good for spending
   Or to give away,

"And all immortal
    Things are sewn
With dreams for thread
    And dreams alone.

"There's a white-hot needle
    Buried in my breast
That stabs and burns me
    And gives no rest;

"I'll thread it with a dream
    And sew my heart whole,
For thread such as that
    I'll give you my soul!"

Then silence fell. . . .
    I looked at the crone
And saw that her face
    Was yellow bone.

I was blind for a moment
    In a whirl of night,
Then my heart grew easy,
    My heart grew light,

And pale as a shark's tooth
    Up came the moon,
I stood all alone
    On the empty dune,

While the needle in my heart
    Began to sew a song;
Softly I hummed it
    As I trudged along.

Marjorie Allen Seiffert

JEZEBEL

WE know she lives upon that thorny hill,
We see her lights and watch her chimneys spark —
But her we have not seen.   The old wives say,
Remembering when she came, her ways were dark,
And that her only name is Jezebel.
One grey idiot tells his tale of love,
Mixing her beauty with the stars of May.

Perhaps we idly wonder if she wore
A flower in her hair, or if the beat
Of her small heels upon the side-walk stone
Was heard at midnight through our lamplit street;
Or why it was she went away to live,
With all her perfumed satin and her lace,
In that wind-beaten, far-off place, alone.

We never wonder more of Jezebel.
We have our work to do and God is hard.
Serving the wheels or guiding straight the plow,
Leaves little thought of frankincense and nard.
Yet, she is like deep waters of the Spring
Running along our minds; down at the roots,
The miracle that makes the April bough.

No man goes near that house above the town.
No man has seen her shadow on the blind,
Though through the night, till dawn, the tallow drips.
But, sometimes, when the chains of duty bind,
Because we reach too eagerly for Heaven,
Sometimes, like little bells within our sleep,
It seems we hear the music of her lips.

Then we have left what we most dearly love,
And momentary lords of Heaven and Hell,

We have gone up through briars and the night,
And seen the secret face of Jezebel.
There, in that still confessional where she waits,
We all have had the blessing of her breast,
As over us she leaned to blow the light.

Up in that room above our godly town,
We have denied the vows we bleed to keep,
We have torn off the lying masks we wear,
And sown without the fear that we must reap.
The young, the pious, and the old, alike
Have been glad penitents upon her heart —
She has absolved us by her kisses, there.

She has forgotten us and let us go,
And we have wakened in our homes again,
To hear the breathing of an earthly bride,
To watch the real world blooming on the pane.
The field, the wheel, the desk, have called once more,
And we have stooped to pick the slender threads
By which we weave the patterns of our pride.

That day, we do not bargain with the sun,
Or curb our pride because one angel fell —
We are the wilful brotherhood who sing!
We bend, without a thought of Jezebel,
Above our work, no longer do we drudge;
We are, awhile, like happy, armoured men
God's searching whip of anger cannot sting!
Scudder Middleton

AN OLD TALE

WHAT shall we say of her,
Who went the path we know of? She is dead —
What shall we say of her?

Men who are very old
Still speak of her.   They say
That she was far too beautiful; they say
Her beauty wrought her ruin.   But they
Are very old.

The old wives break their threads, they shake their
       heads.
They shake their heads when men will speak of her;
They say she was too beautiful.

I must not think of her, I must
Not speak of her!   My mother says
One should not think of her.

She went the path we knew of; she is dead.
They say few knew her truly while she lived,
Though men will speak of her.

It really does not matter she is dead —
One need not think of her.   Although one night
Folks heard her weeping, yet beside a pool
One moonlit springtime I could swear she sang!

But she is dead — one must not think of her.
                        Marya Zaturensky

HERE LIES A LADY

HERE lies a lady of beauty and high degree.
Of chills and fever she died, of fever and chills,
The delight of her husband, her aunts, an infant of
       three,
And of medicos marvelling sweetly on her ills.

For either she burned, and her confident eyes would
    blaze,
And her fingers fly in a manner to puzzle their heads —
What was she making?   Why, nothing; she sat in a
    maze
Of old scraps of laces, snipped into curious shreds —

Or this would pass, and the light of her fire decline
Till she lay discouraged and cold as a thin stalk white
    and blown,
And would not open her eyes, to kisses, to wine;
The sixth of these states was her last; the cold settled
    down.

Sweet ladies, long may ye bloom, and toughly I hope
    ye may thole,
But was she not lucky?   In flowers and lace and
    mourning,
In love and great honour we bade God rest her soul
After six little spaces of chill, and six of burning.

                John Crowe Ransom

GHOSTLY REAPER

Now while the wind is up I hear
A dark scythe swung in air,
A door creaks by the crooked elm —
Who is reaping there?

Who goes to cut the field tonight
Beside the lily pond?
Who comes to swing a rusty scythe
From Limbo, or beyond?

                Harold Vinal

THE SILVER CANOE

THE pack is too hard on the shoulders,
   The feet are too slow on the trail;
The log that was blazing, but smolders,
   And gone is the zest from the tale.

Then why should we wistfully tarry,
   Old comrades, grown feeble and few?
Come, rest on the shore of the carry
   And wait for the Silver Canoe.

The Silver Canoe — and who guesses
   What paddle is plied at the stern?
It comes in the silence that blesses
   Through forests of cedar and fern;

It comes when the twilight is fading
   Through shadow to moonlight, and then
It goes with its earth-weary lading
   From moonlight to shadow again.

It glides to a lake in the mountains
   As blue as the skies that are fair
And fed by the purest of fountains,
   A lake of the woodlands; and there,

Oh, pathfinder, cragsman, frontiersman,
   Your cabin is ready for you;
For peace is the goal of the Steersman,
   The bourne of the Silver Canoe.

Arthur Guiterman

THE GHOSTLY GALLEY

WHEN comes the ghostly galley
　　Whose rowers dip the oar
Without a sound to startle us,
　　Unheeding on the shore, —

If they should beckon you aboard
　　Before they beckon me,
How could I bear the waiting time
　　Till I should put to sea!

Jessie B. Rittenhouse

RESURGENCE

I HAVE so loved you I can never find
Rest from the thought of you in any place.
Far have I left your cypress-bed behind,
But not your hand's light touch; but not your face.
Only this moment did a voice contrive
To make hope start up, quivering. I drew
Close to the sound of it: you were alive
A little space with laughter blowing through.
You were alive and then you were more dead
Than ever you had been through all the years.
I heard a voice and knew not what it said:
Some simple trifle meant for other ears.
No one to share this exile and this pain;
No one to know that you have died again.

Margaret Tod Ritter

AUT CAESAR, AUT NULLUS

"COME! Sun and laughter wait us at the end."
You whisper as I walk a darkened road
Bowed with my burden. God grows kind to send
A guide who leads me from this crushing load.

. . . No further! He is beautiful, the dead,
Thrust from my heart; so empty now and free —
I must go back. . . . It aches still where his head
Long pressed against my bosom, heavily.

Lilian White Spencer

THERE WILL BE STARS

THERE will be stars over the place forever;
   Though the house we loved and the street we loved
      are lost,
Every time the earth circles her orbit
   On the night the autumn equinox is crossed,
Two stars we knew, poised on the peak of midnight
   Will reach their zenith; stillness will be deep;
There will be stars over the place forever,
   There will be stars forever, while we sleep.

Sara Teasdale

ALL WILL BE WELL

ALL will be well with me for I remember
Days out of April and nights out of June,
And I have filched from patient-eyed September
Moments like flowers and hours like a tune:
For what is living but a noble jesting?
And what is parting but a kingly mirth?
And heaven, perhaps, is just October resting
After the months when Hymen walked the earth.

Amory Hare

AS IN A PICTURE-BOOK

My mother died when I was young,
  Yet not too young to know
What terror round the dark halls clung
  That aching day of snow.

I knew she could not comfort me.
  I sat there all alone.
Cold sorrow held me quietly
  Dumb as a winter stone.

And yet I seemed to watch it all
  As in a picture-book:
The silent people in the hall,
  My father's frozen look, —

The heaped white roses, and my dress
  So very black and new.
I watched it without weariness. . . .
  Ah, how the snow-blast blew!
    . . . .

Tonight you say you love me : — me, —
  Who leap to love you.   Lo,
I am all yours so utterly
  You need not speak, nor show

One sign, but I shall understand
  Out to our life's last rim :
Out into death's uncertain land,
  Gracious be it or grim.

I am all yours. . . . And yet tonight
  The old trick haunts me.   Look!
I see your face, O new delight,
  As in a picture-book.

Your face, your shape, the fire-lit room,
   The red rose on the shelf, —
And, leaning to its passionate bloom,
   Troubled with love, myself. . . .

Oh, hold your hand across my eyes.
   They have no right to see!
But now, as then, they are too wise.
   They stare.   They frighten me.

                              Fannie Stearns Davis

THE SENSE OF DEATH

Since I have felt the sense of death,
   Since I have borne its dread, its fear,
   Oh, how my life has grown more dear!
Since I have felt the sense of death.
   Sorrows are good and cares are small,
   Since I have known the loss of all.

Since I have felt the sense of death,
   And death forever at my side,
   Oh, how the world has opened wide!
Since I have felt the sense of death.
   My hours are jewels that I spend,
   For I have seen the hours end.

Since I have felt the sense of death,
   Since I have looked on that black night,
   My inmost brain is fierce with light!
Since I have felt the sense of death.
   O dark that made my eyes to see, —
   O death that gave my life to me!

                              Helen Hoyt

REALITY

My life is crowned by three consummate things:
Love that may worship, blind though unafraid,
Some fictive being that the mind has made;
The spread and beat of bold creation's wings
When, poised above the blast, the spirit sings;
The moment when the storms of matter fade
And, clear as cloud-washed heavens, are displayed
Replies to our bewildered questionings.
No magi brought these treasures from afar;
They were engendered by that inner lord,
The dungeoned mind, the veritable me
Who, when the prison gateway swung ajar,
Pressed, like the pallid woman in the horde,
To touch the hem of white reality.

Robert Haven Schauffler

ONE SHALL BE TAKEN AND THE OTHER LEFT

There is no Rachel any more
And so it does not really matter.
Leah alone is left, and she
Goes her own way inscrutably.
Soft-eyed she goes, content to scatter
Fine sand along a barren shore
Where there was sand enough before:
Or from a well that has no water
Raising a futile pitcher up
Lifts to her lips an empty cup.
Now she is Laban's only daughter:
There is no Rachel any more.

Aline Kilmer

ANN RUTLEDGE

SHE came like music: when she went
    A silence fell upon the man.
Death took the sun away with her —
    Ann Rutledge — deathless Ann.

She left upon his life a light,
    A music sounding through his years,
A spirit singing through his toils,
    A memory in his tears.

She was the dream within his dream;
    And when she turned and went away
She took the romance from the night,
    The rapture from the day.

But from her beauty and her doom,
    A man rose merciful and just;
And a great People still can feel
    The passion of her dust.

Edwin Markham

SONG FROM A MASQUE

BACK where the Old Gods dream there is no pain;
    There is no grief, back where the Old Gods sleep;
There is no pride nor pity nor disdain,
    And none to weep:

There is no fear to hunt the hours away,
    There is no hope to hound the tired heart on,
Only a twilight that shall ever stay,
    With no dream gone;

Only old mirth, the shadow of a sound,
  Only old love, the shadow of a fire,
Soft as the brown leaf flutters to the ground,
  Echo desire:

Back where the Old Gods dream there is no pain,
  There is no grief, back where the Old Gods sleep;
There is no pride nor pity nor disdain,
  And none to weep.

                                   Margaret Widdemer

NUIT BLANCHE

I WANT no horns to rouse me up to-night,
And trumpets make too clamorous a ring
To fit my mood, it is so weary white
I have no wish for doing any thing.

A music coaxed from humming strings would please;
Not plucked, but drawn in creeping cadences
Across a sunset wall where some Marquise
Picks a pale rose amid strange silences.

Ghostly and vaporous her gown sweeps by
The twilight dusking wall, I hear her feet
Delaying on the gravel, and a sigh
Briefly permitted, touches the air like sleet.

And it is dark, I hear her feet no more.
A red moon leers beyond the lily-tank.
A drunken moon ogling a sycamore,
Running long fingers down its shining flank.

A lurching moon, as nimble as a clown,
Cuddling the flowers and trees which burn like glass.
Red, kissing lips, I feel you on my gown —
Kiss me, red lips, and then pass — pass.

Music, you are pitiless to-night.
And I so old, so cold, so languorously white.

Amy Lowell

FLASH

I AM less of myself and more of the sun;
The beat of life is wearing me
To an incomplete oblivion,
Yet not to the certain dignity
Of death.   *They cannot even die
Who have not lived.*

The hungry jaws
Of space snap at my unlearned eye,
And time tears in my flesh like claws.

If I am not life's, if I am not death's,
Out of chaos I must re-reap
The burden of untasted breaths.
Who has not waked may not yet sleep.

Hazel Hall

HERO'S INVOCATION TO DEATH

I WHO have no lover —
Swift winds make me over!

Tear my torch asunder,
Stamp its pale beams under;

Scourge me with your lashes;
Where your legion crashes
Let my grief be vented,
Ravening, demented.

I who have no lover —
Swift winds make me over!

I who have no lover —
Cold waves make me over!

Bear me, being mortal,
To some sheltered portal;
Spread a blue-green billow
For our marriage pillow;
Wrap me round with tidal
Samite for my bridal.

I who have no lover —
Cold waves make me over!

Margaret Tod Ritter

SEA SORROW

(Lament for Conory Mor)

LENT lily, pasque flower, herb trinity,
A bridal wreath for the white-armed sea,
        Here is loneliness,
        Here is lamentation.

My sorrow on the sea — it is Morna sings,
Striking her harp with the silver strings,
My sorrow on the sea — it is Conory's queen,
Morna, raising her voice to keen;
        Here is loneliness,
        Here is lamentation.

My sorrow on her whose cool hands lift
Conory's curls to the deep sea drift;
    Here is loneliness,
    Here is lamentation.

My sorrow on her whose salt kiss lies
On the burning beauty of Conory's eyes,
My sorrow on her whose green veils form
His winding-sheet where the fishes swarm;
    Here is loneliness,
    Here is lamentation.

My sorrow on the flowers strewn to the wave,
Lent lily, samite for a king's grave,
    Here is loneliness,
    Here is lamentation.

My sorrow on pasque flower, purple and vair,
Royal colors for a king to wear,
My sorrow on trinity-herb's green leaf,
May the Holy Three console my grief!
    Here is loneliness,
    Here is lamentation.

Lent lily, pasque flower, herb trinity,
Sea Bride, unending my keen shall be;
    Here is loneliness,
    Here is lamentation.
        Rose Mills Powers

SONG

WE cannot die, for loveliness
    Is an eternal thing.
If God, his dim old eyes to bless,
    Brings back the Spring,

Shall He not bring again your grace,
    Your laughter, your warm hair?
And how can He destroy my face
    Your kiss made fair?
              Mary Carolyn Davies

WHAT IF SOME LOVER IN A FAR–OFF SPRING

WHAT if some lover in a far-off spring,
Down the long passage of a hundred years,
Should breathe his longing through the words I sing —
And close the book, dazed by a woman's tears?
Does it mean aught to you that such might be?
Ah! We far-seekers! Solely thus were proved
From dream to deed the souls of you and me; —
Thus only were it real that we had loved.
Grey ghosts blcwn down the desolate moors of time!
Poor wanderers, lost to any hope of rest!
Joined by the measure of a faltering rhyme!
Sundered by deep division of the breast! —
Sundered by all wherein we both have part;
Joined by the far world-seeking of each heart.
              Arthur Davison Ficke

THINGS

THINGS that are lovely
    Can tear my heart in two —
Moonlight on still pools,
    You.

Things that are tender
    Can fill me with delight —
Old songs remembered,
    Night.

Things that are lonely
   Can make me catch my breath —
The hunger for lost arms. . . .
   Death.

Dorothy Dow

ALONG THE WIND

I

SHE was a wild, wild song, and she is gone.
Her eyes were all the stars that fire the night.
Her thoughts were harebells on an Alpine height
Ungathered, and her laughter was the dawn.
She held me as the sky holds up the stars
With tenderness, and for love's way she drew
An orbit beautiful around the blue
Where light breaks through the cordoning mortal bars.

Oh, do not say her sweetness will survive,
Like Christian glory overcoming Rome's,
Or maidenhair grown in the catacombs.
These are poor words for me, alone, alive
Upon the world, so small it set her free —
Now grown a desert, vast and bleak to me.

II

Sometimes I think my grief a mean pretense.
When all amazed, I wake from sight to stare
At what she was, and feel again her hair
Across my eyes with a gold effluence
From streams beyond the springs of mind and sense,
And harmony and wisdom everywhere:
There comes a startled word, a sudden flare
Of truth from old divine embodiments.

I shrink, too weak to be unreconciled,
Till, a submissive Lilliputian, on
The ground I draw the eyes of Acteon;
And I draw Aphrodite, when she smiled
Swiftly on young Anchises, and was gone,
Leaving him very old, and mute, and mild.

Chard Powers Smith

A LOVER FOR DEATH

Oh, who will find a lover for Death and for her only?
  Though all men kiss her lips, they kiss against
      their will.
Oh, pity Death! Wistful, she is, and exquisite and
      lonely
  And all who sleep with her lie curiously still.

Ralph Cheyney

THEY SLEEP SO QUIETLY

They sleep so quietly, those English dead,
In Bruton churchyard, when the cold wind sighs
Through the stripped branches, weaving overhead
Fantastic webs against the wintry skies.
They do not heed the hurrying snow which covers
Their unremembered names, — Margaret, and Joan,
Philip and Lucy, long forgotten lovers, —
Where the white silence of the drifts is blown.

But when the hawthorn spills her petals down,
And ranks of jonquils break in shining blooms
As April lingers in the little town,
They will lie dreaming in the ancient tombs
Of Cornwall's cliffs beneath the soft spring rains,
Or foxgloves nodding in the Devon lanes.

Virginia Lyne Tunstall

THE LAST SLEEP

SOME shining April I shall be asleep,
  And over me the ancient joy shall pass;
I shall not see young Spring dance down the world
  With ribbons of green grass.

But I shall dream of all that I have lost —
  Breath of the wind, immortal loveliness,
Wild beauty of the sunlight on the hills,
  Now mine no less

Because I slumber.   Nay, but more than mine,
  Since I a part of them shall strangely be. . . .
Only, I ask, when the pink hawthorn breaks,
  That one shall think of me.

Charles Hanson Towne

I WOULD REMEMBER CONSTANT THINGS

THE little broken bones of men,
  They ride on every wind that blows,
With dust of Memphis whirled again
  And this year's dust of last year's rose;
The little bitter tears of men,
  They are but drops in the salt sea,
Lost forever beyond all ken
  Of flesh like you and me.

And though from mountains worn away
  I mix the mortar for my house
And build within the light of day
  For studious ease and long carouse.

The rain shall beat above my head,
　　The wind shall rattle my bolted door,
And all the ghosts of all the dead
　　Shall pace my fire-lit floor.

Yet I shall fashion greater Gods
　　For Lares, now, than other men;
I would forget how Sirius plods
　　Through galaxies and back again;
I would remember constant things,
　　As sleep whereof no dreams affray,
Before the wind on wandering wings
　　Has blown my bones away.

J. U. Nicholson

OMNIA EXEUNT IN MYSTERIUM

How dumb the vanished billions who have died!
　　With backward gaze conjectural we wait,
　　And ere the invading Shadow penetrate,
The echo from a mighty heart that cried
Is made a sole memorial to pride.
　　From out that night's inscrutable estate,
　　A few cold voices wander, desolate
With all that love has lost or grief has sighed.

Slaves, seamen, captains, councillors and kings,
　　Gone utterly, save for those echoes far!
　　As they before, I tread a forfeit land,
Till the supreme and ancient silence flings
　　Its pall between the dreamer and the star.
　　O desert wide!　O little grain of sand!

George Sterling

LET ME GO DOWN TO DUST

LET me go down to dust and dreams
Gently, O Lord, with never a fear
Of death beyond the day that is done;
In such a manner as beseems
A kinsman of the wild, a son
Of stoic earth whose race is run.
Let me go down as any deer,
Who, broken by a desperate flight,
Sinks down to slumber for the night —
Dumbly serene in certitude
That it will rise again at dawn,
Buoyant, refreshed of limb, renewed,
And confident that it will thrill
To-morrow to its nuzzling fawn,
To the bugle-notes of elk upon the hill.

Let me go down to dreams and dust
Gently, O Lord, with quiet trust
And the fortitude that marks a child
Of earth, a kinsman of the wild.
Let me go down as any doe
That nods upon its ferny bed,
And, lulled to slumber by the flow
Of talking water, the muffled brawl
Of far cascading waterfall,
At last lets down its weary head
Deep in the brookmints in the glen;
And under the starry-candled sky,
With never the shadow of a sigh,
Gives its worn body back to earth again.

Lew Sarett

MENTIS TRIST

Never fear the phantom bird
Meditating in the Fens,
Night will come and quench your eyes,
Blind at last like other men's;
Never fear the tales you heard
In the rhetoric of lies.

Nothing here will challenge you,
Not the heron, tall and white,
Countersign upon the edge
Of the waterfall of night.
This is Avalon's canoe,
Eden murmurs in the sedge.

Here.   My hand in pledge of rest.
Drift at random, all is well.
Twilight is a slow lagoon,
Dark will be a citadel.
Travelers who know the west
But report the waning moon.

In the citadel of peace
Hang the trophies of the world,
Yet no barons don their mail,
And no pennant is unfurled.
Daily robe, the Golden Fleece,
Daily cup, the Holy Grail.

Robert Hillyer

CALL HIM HIGH SHELLEY NOW

Here lies a frigid man whom men deplore,
A presence concentrated in a frame,
A full-length portrait of the flesh of yore,
A still-life study of a death aflame,

White, unresistant, intimate and free,
The eyes a secret, hands as cold as stars,
A man who lies with his biography,
A dreaming book whose wounds have dried to scars :
There flies a thrilling soul men cultivate,
A ghostly eagle solving mysteries,
His darkest faults, graces they emulate,
Wings redolent of suns and eyes of seas :
For they who shrank from his mad human ache
Call him high Shelley now and praise his wake.

Alfred Kreymborg

COOL TOMBS

WHEN Abraham Lincoln was shoveled into the
    tombs, he forgot the copperheads and the
    assassin . . . in the dust, in the cool tombs.

And Ulysses Grant lost all thought of con men and
    Wall Street, cash and collateral turned ashes
    . . . in the dust, in the cool tombs.

Pocahontas' body, lovely as a poplar, sweet as a red
    haw in November or a pawpaw in May, did she
    wonder ? does she remember ? . . . in the dust,
    in the cool tombs ?

Take any streetful of people buying clothes and
    groceries, cheering a hero or throwing confetti
    and blowing tin horns . . . tell me if the
    lovers are losers . . . tell me if any get more
    than the lovers . . . in the dust . . . in the
    cool tombs.

Carl Sandburg

A RHYME OUT OF MOTLEY

"I GRASPED a thread of silver; it cut me to the bone —
I reached for an apple; it was bleak as a stone —
I reached for a heart, and touched a raw blade —
And this was the bargain God had made
For a little gift of speech
Set a cubit higher than the common reach,
A debt running on until the fool is dead."

Carve a Pater Noster to put at his head ʻ
As a curse or a prayer,
And leave him there.

Amy Lowell

FANTASY IN PURPLE

BEAT the drums of tragedy for me.
Beat the drums of tragedy and death.
And let the choir sing a stormy song
To drown the rattle of my dying breath.

Beat the drums of tragedy for me,
And let the white violins whir thin and slow,
But blow one blaring trumpet note of sun
To go with me
            to the darkness
                        where I go.

Langston Hughes

EPITHALAMIUM AND ELEGY

MY single constancy is love of life:
Because we have entered no such formal pact
As dulls devotion between man and wife,
No bland acknowledgment, no binding fact,

No mingling of betrothal with divorce,
No dated bliss, no midnight certitude,
No sad necessity, no matter of course,
No pallid answer saying why we wooed;
Because she lets me love her as I can
Moment by moment, moments that always come
Beyond the calculation of a man
For joy or pain, for epithalamium
Or for elegy, and because, when I am spent,
Life shall have had her way, shall be content
Still to confer the sweet bewilderment
On someone else, shall loosen her lovely hair
To the wind, shall turn with bountiful intent
Toward anyone at all, and I not there,
Shall offer cool papayas, pale bamboo
And amorous guava to a later comer,
And none of her gifts, not even a drop of dew,
To me who had received them many a summer.
These are not harlotries but only joy,
These are the very tiptoes of delight.
This is the happiness she gives a boy
With nothing of wickedness, nothing of spite
In that immense, delicious, naked bed
Where anyone may lie, except the dead. . . .
But I shall leave her.   All that there is of rest
Shall be little enough, after so much of love.
Wherever I move, she is there.   Her open breast
Offers the tenderness I am dying of.
Her arm along my body like a snake
Has softly wound me into rings of sleep
And, every time again, stings me awake
And drowns me in her rhythms deep and deep. . . .
Can I be tragical, in having had
My love of life by life herself subdued?

Since I am satiate with joy, can I be sad
In leaving?   All that there is of solitude
Shall be little enough, after this vast embrace.
Give her some younger lover in my place.

Witter Bynner

SONNETS FROM " TWO LIVES"

THIS afternoon on Willow-Walk alone
I wandered from my desk and books away :
The crew was in the shell upon the bay,
Eight slanting backs, the coach with megaphone
Aft in his launch; a girl upon a roan
Went cantering by me, with a cherry-spray
For riding whip. . . .   Three years ago to-day. . . .
Still clings the flesh in coffin to the bone?
Then, as I gazed across the flashing May,
Strangely I yearned again to boyhood hills,
Where, sitting on the sagging pasture bars,
I'd watch the moon on windrows of the hay,
And whistle to the answering whippoorwills,
And wonder at the history of the stars.

Death hath two hands to slay with : with the one
He stabs the loveliness of Yesterday,
Till all its gold and blue is sodden gray
To memory forever, in the sun :
Think ye I think upon our earliest kiss,
Our walks, our vines, our readings, as I would
Were she still by me in her womanhood
To join in tender talk on all of this?
Death hath two hands to slay with : with the other
He stabs the glory of our bright Tomorrow —
Our best reality, our younger brother,
Our spirit-self — upon the fields of sorrow :

Think ye he took no unbuilt house from me,
No unsailed voyage with her across the sea?

Thrice summer and autumn passed into the west,
Across her grave with flower and leaf they passed,
Thrice winter with his moon.   Now spring at last —
The fatal spring of her supreme unrest
And ultimate hour — its green young feet hath pressed
Once more on hills and fields and brought to us
From southern oceans small birds amorous
To build in trees of song the happy nest
Above her grave. . . .   And meanwhile in the world
Fire, flood, and whirlwind smote the planted ground,
And ships with lights and music sank at sea,
And flags o'er new-born nations were unfurled,
And men discovered, as the earth went round,
New stars off yonder in eternity.

William Ellery Leonard

LONGING

I DID not wish eternity;
    A briefer season would suffice
For loving sun and sky and sea
    And Spring's new-blossomed Paradise.

I could have been content to take
    A limited delight in snows,
In midnight stars and gray daybreak,
    And the warm wonder of the rose.

But when I add you to the score
    Of sun and sky and sea and Spring,
My heart cries out in pain for more
    Hours for our golden journeying.

If ache and cry can work their will,
 Time will not end for you — for me —
Till you and I have lingered still
 An unbelieved eternity.

     Clement Wood

LOVE SONG

THE delicate silver gates are closed, the road ahead
 is paved with swords,
There's only the comfort of your breast, the arm's
 strength, and gentle words
To meet the foam of the black stars a stinging wind
 flings in our faces;
A bare room is the day's end, and a hard bed for our
 bodies' places.

The tired limb, and the tight brow, and the strong
 clasp of a hand hardened —
Only these, now the rose has gone, one with the years
 that life pardoned
When your blue eyes that love deepened were more
 merry and less brave,
Only these are ours, my dear, for what we give and
 what we gave.

Yet only now that our eyes have seen there is no star
 on the hills ahead
To guide through the ways that all have known, yet
 none could mark, of men dead —
O only now, my dear, have we known the sole answer
 to love's need:
The heart's dream, and the heart's strength, and the
 light shed where the feet bleed.

     George Brandon Saul

TOGETHER

You and I by this lamp with these
Few books shut out the world.   Our knees
Touch almost in this little space.
But I am glad.   I see your face.
The silences are long, but each
Hears the other without speech.
And in this simple scene there is
The essence of all subtleties,
The freedom from all fret and smart,
The one sure sabbath of the heart.

The world — we cannot conquer it,
Nor change the mind of fools one whit.
Here, here alone do we create
Beauty and peace inviolate;
Here night by night and hour by hour
We build a high impregnable tower
Whence may shine, now and again,
A light to light the feet of men
When they see the rays thereof :
And this is marriage, this is love.

Ludwig Lewisohn

THERE STRETCH BETWEEN US WONDER–WOVEN BONDS

There stretch between us wonder-woven bonds,
Fine as a thread but strong as braided steel, —
A link that to each changing need responds,
Nor binds the butterfly upon the wheel.
For the coarse bondage sanctioned of men's law
I   would   not,   though   I   could,   these   gossamers
        change, —

Give time and circumstance that leave to draw
Closer the net till nearness must estrange!
And yet a longing restless in me burns
To lock what never might the lock endure: —
As a glad sailor, sea-impassioned, yearns
That what he loves for being unsure, were sure, —
That the fierce doubtful splendor of bright foam
Might somehow, fierce and doubtful, light him home.

Arthur Davison Ficke

EPITHALAMION

Come now, though Muses are not left to sing
In sweet and pagan names the day of love,
Though ancient rites escape our fostering,
And boys and girls may take no blossom trove
From April boughs whereof
Garlands we plucked when youth was at its spring;
Though viol and rebeck may no longer play
For largesse of this morn, nor dancers move
With music to the house where we must stay,
Yet Love, awake, for still it is our bridal day.

Awake and come to windows where the night
Is gone and takes the storm, the powerful spell
That once it worked on us, but now delight
Kindles the tongue of every morning bell.
Awake and answer well
With thy red lips and all thy lovely might.
Enclose me with thine arms and kiss away
Old fevers that we breathed in love's despite,
And breathe a world where we can longer stay,
And wake, my Love, for still it is our bridal day.

Open the door whereat my love will go
To this the festival so long ordained.
Let be the music that ye long have feigned
For bridals that ye know,
And let the hills another music sound
From old and stubborn ground.
Let the long street a solemn music speak
And larger beauties break
From this wide world that is our marriage room,
And April grass and every April bloom,
And Hymen cry and now your joyance make,
And drink the skies' sweet influence while ye may.
Go forth, my Love, for still it is our bridal day.

Donald Davidson

THE FLIGHT

WE are two eagles
Flying together
Under the heavens,
Over the mountains,
Stretched on the wind.
Sunlight heartens us,
Blind snow baffles us,
Clouds wheel after us
Ravelled and thinned.

We are like eagles,
But when Death harries us,
Human and humbled
When one of us goes,
Let the other follow,
Let the flight be ended,
Let the fire blacken,
Let the book close.

Sara Teasdale

MY LIGHT WITH YOURS

WHEN the sea has devoured the ships,
And the spires and the towers
Have gone back to the hills,
And all the cities
Are one with the plains again,
And the beauty of bronze
And the strength of steel
Are blown over silent continents,
As the desert sand is blown —
My dust with yours forever.

When folly and wisdom are no more,
And fire is no more,
Because man is no more;
When the dead world slowly spinning
Drifts and falls through the void —
My light with yours
In the Light of Lights forever!

Edgar Lee Masters

ENVOI   (1919)

Go, dumb-born book,
Tell her that sang me once that song of Lawes:
Hadst thou but song
As thou hast subjects known,
Then were there cause in thee that should condone
Even my faults that heavy upon me lie,
And build her glories their longevity.

Tell her that sheds
Such treasure in the air,
Recking naught else but that her graces give
Life to the moment,

I would bid them live
As roses might, in magic amber laid,
Red overwrought with orange and all made
One substance and one colour
Braving time.

Tell her that goes
With song upon her lips
But sings not out the song, nor knows
The maker of it, some other mouth,
May be as fair as hers,
Might, in new ages, gain her worshippers,
When our two dusts with Waller's shall be laid,
Siftings on siftings in oblivion,
Till change hath broken down
All things save Beauty alone.

Ezra Pound

INDEX OF AUTHORS

INDEX OF FIRST LINES